ISBN 952-5216-00-4 (the series)
ISBN 952-5216-01-2 (book 1)

Published by Fapet Oy
(Fapet Oy, PO BOX 14, FIN-00131 HELSINKI, FINLAND)

Copyright © 1998 by Fapet Oy. All rights reserved.

Printed by Gummerus Oy, Jyväskylä, Finland 1998

 Printed on LumiMatt 100 g/m^2, Enso Fine Papers Oy, Imatra Mills

Papermaking Science and Technology

a series of 19 books covering the latest technology and future trends

Book 1

Economics of the Pulp and Paper Industry

Series editors
Johan Gullichsen, Helsinki University of Technology
Hannu Paulapuro, Helsinki University of Technology

Book editor
Magnus Diesen, Enso Oyj

Series reviewer
Brian Attwood, St. Anne's Paper and Paperboard Co. Ltd

Book reviewer
E. Carlyle Franklin, North Carolina State University

TAPPI PRESS

Published in cooperation with the Finnish Paper Engineers' Association and TAPPI

Foreword

Johan Gullichsen and Hannu Paulapuro

PAPERMAKING SCIENCE AND TECHNOLOGY

Papermaking is a vast, multidisciplinary technology that has expanded tremendously in recent years. Significant advances have been made in all areas of papermaking, including raw materials, production technology, process control and end products. The complexity of the processes, the scale of operation and production speeds leave little room for error or malfunction. Modern papermaking would not be possible without a proper command of a great variety of technologies, in particular advanced process control and diagnostic methods. Not only has the technology progressed and new technology emerged, but our understanding of the fundamentals of unit processes, raw materials and product properties has also deepened considerably. The variations in the industry's heterogeneous raw materials, and the sophistication of pulping and papermaking processes require a profound understanding of the mechanisms involved. Paper and board products are complex in structure and contain many different components. The requirements placed on the way these products perform are wide, varied and often conflicting. Those involved in product development will continue to need a profound understanding of the chemistry and physics of both raw materials and product structures.

Paper has played a vital role in the cultural development of mankind. It still has a key role in communication and is needed in many other areas of our society. There is no doubt that it will continue to have an important place in the future. Paper must, however, maintain its competitiveness through continuous product development in order to meet the ever-increasing demands on its performance. It must also be produced economically by environment-friendly processes with the minimum use of resources. To meet these challenges, everyone working in this field must seek solutions by applying the basic sciences of engineering and economics in an integrated, multidisciplinary way.

The Finnish Paper Engineers' Association has previously published textbooks and handbooks on pulping and papermaking. The last edition appeared in the early 80's. There is now a clear need for a new series of books. It was felt that the new series should provide more comprehensive coverage of all aspects of papermaking science and technology. Also, that it should meet the need for an academic-level textbook and at the same time serve as a handbook for production and management people working in this field. The result is this series of 19 volumes, which is also available as a CD-ROM.

When the decision was made to publish the series in English, it was natural to seek the assistance of an international organization in this field. TAPPI was the obvious partner as it is very active in publishing books and other educational material on pulping and papermaking. TAPPI immediately understood the significance of the suggested new series, and readily agreed to assist. As most of the contributors to the series are Finnish, TAPPI provided North American reviewers for each volume in the series. Mr. Brian Attwood was appointed overall reviewer for the series as a whole. His input is gratefully acknowledged. We thank TAPPI and its representatives for their valuable contribution throughout the project. Thanks are also due to all TAPPI-appointed reviewers, whose work has been invaluable in finalizing the text and in maintaining a high standard throughout the series.

A project like this could never have succeeded without contributors of the very highest standard. Their motivation, enthusiasm and the ability to produce the necessary material in a reasonable time has made our work both easy and enjoyable. We have also learnt a lot in our "own field" by reading the excellent manuscripts for these books.

We also wish to thank FAPET (Finnish American Paper Engineers' Textbook), which is handling the entire project. We are especially obliged to Ms. Mari Barck, the project coordinator. Her devotion, patience and hard work have been instrumental in getting the project completed on schedule.

Finally, we wish to thank the following companies for their financial support:

A. Ahlstrom Corporation

Enso Oyj

Kemira Oy

Metsä-Serla Corporation

Rauma Corporation

Raisio Chemicals Ltd

Tamfelt Corporation

UPM-Kymmene Corporation

We are confident that this series of books will find its way into the hands of numerous students, paper engineers, production and mill managers and even professors. For those who prefer the use of electronic media, the CD-ROM form will provide all that is contained in the printed version. We anticipate they will soon make paper copies of most of the material.

List of Contributors

Magnus Diesen, M.Sc., Senior Vice President, Enso Oyj

Preface
Magnus Diesen

The aim of this book is to provide a global perspective on the following issues from a Scandinavian - more particularly a Finnish - viewpoint.

1. Information on forest industry raw material resources, markets, as well as the worldwide structure and various strategies of the industry.

2. Ability to evaluate the economic consequences of decisions taken in a pulp or paper mill.

3. Ability to analyse and compare the profitability and competitiveness of the forest industries in different countries.

4. Ability to analyse alternative investments with different criteria and to select the best alternative in a given situation.

It is assumed, that the reader has basic knowledge about the pulp and paper industry.

This book was written in 1996 and early 1997. Thus the sources of information used and referred to contained data up to that time, in most cases up to and including 1995.

Jaakko Poyry Consulting Oy provided a major part of the data and information in this book. My employer, Enso Oyj, encouraged and supported me, and my colleagues have contributed valuable and well-structured comments.

I want to thank you all.

Helsinki, February 1998

Table of Contents

1. Main characteristics of the global forest industry 10
2. Impact of the forest industry on the economy of Finland 21
3. Raw material resources – wood supply 30
4. Raw material resources – secondary fiber supply 48
5. World paper markets 61
6. Structure of the global forest industry and main suppliers in the mid 1990s 77
7. Cost structure and management accounting 102
8. Investment decision 127
9. Economy of scale 141
10. Economy of integration 152
11. The impact of currency exchange rates on competitiveness 160
12. Future strategies for the Scandinavian forest industry 175

    Glossary 180

    Conversion factors 185

    Index 186

CHAPTER 1

Main characteristics of the global forest industry

1	**General**	10
2	**Typical features of the forest industry**	11
2.1	Growth	11
2.2	Technical development	11
2.3	Concentration	13
2.4	Cyclical nature of the forest industry	13
2.5	High investment rates	14
3	**Opportunities for the forest industry**	15
4	**Threats to the forest industry**	16
	Sources	19

CHAPTER 1

Main characteristics of the global forest industry

1 General

Paper is an important commodity for mankind at the end of the twentieth century. Its importance is steadily increasing. Global paper consumption reached 260 million tons in 1995. Approximately 45% of this amount was used for communication – newsprint and printing and writing papers, 40% for packaging – mainly liner, fluting and boxboards, and the remaining 15% for miscellaneous purposes such as hygienic, health care and other specialized purposes.

The paper industry is large and growing. Table 1 shows the paper industry turnover in Europe compared with certain other industrial sectors[1].

Table 1. Paper industry turnover compared to other industrial sectors in European Union countries.

	Billion ECU
Glass	24
Paper	43
Communications & electronics	49
Pharmaceutical	65

The paper industry generates wealth both through its growth and its unusually steep employment pyramid. Figure 1 shows the components of the pyramid[1].

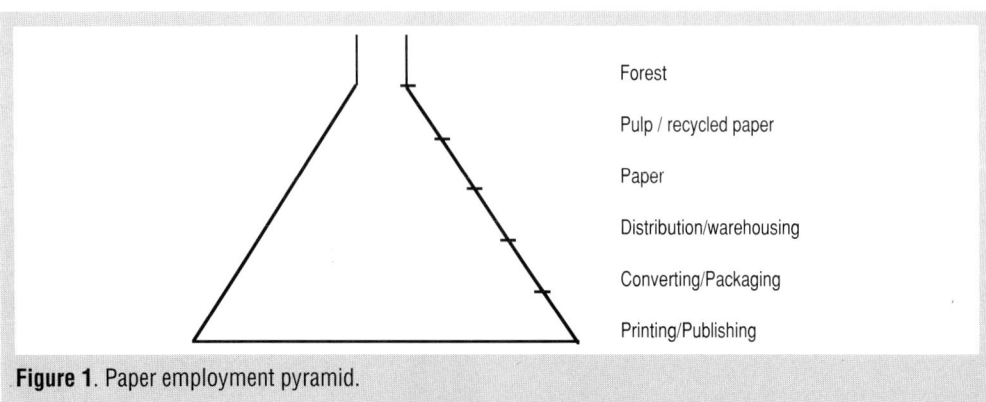

Figure 1. Paper employment pyramid.

Many other industrial segments participate in the employment pyramid including transportation, the printing industry, the converting industry for boxes, laminates, etc. Equipment manufacturers and chemical suppliers also participate. Consider as an example that the top part of the pyramid is a pulp mill. A modern pulp mill employs approximately 300 persons. Considering the indirect influence on forestry, logging, transportation, equipment and chemicals, etc., the multiplier effect is approximately estimated to be 11. The total employment effect of a modern pulp mill is therefore approximately 3300[2].

2 Typical features of the forest industry

2.1 Growth

The total production of the paper industry has grown globally from less than 10 million tons in 1900 through 43 million tons in 1950 to 260 million tons in 1995. Since 1950, the average annual growth has been 4.1%.

Table 2 compares the growth in Europe to certain other industries.

Table 2. Average annual industrial growth rate 1980–1993.

	%/a
Paper	3.3
Chemicals	2.5
GDP	2.1
Manufacturing	1.1

The fact that the growth of demand has exceeded Gross Domestic Production (GDP) growth by a factor of 1.5 has been the decisive driving force of this development. It has stimulated use of new technology in combination with new investments and has accelerated the investment level. This has contributed to newer and more modern production facilities and closure of old, uncompetitive mills and machines.

2.2 Technical development

Progress in technical matters has been enormous. For example, Table 3 shows the development in speed and width of paper machines for newsprint.

CHAPTER 1

Table 3. Speed and width development of new newsprint machines since 1900.

	1900	1960	1995	2000 est.
Max. speed m/min	200	800	1600	1900
Max. width m	3	7	9–9.5	9–9.5

The above table indicates that the maximum width of paper machines will not exceed the present 9.5 m value in the near future and will remain at this level. Speed has increased dramatically and will probably continue to do so for at least the next ten years. A new pilot paper machine at Valmet, Rautpohja inaugurated early in 1996 has a maximum speed of 2500 m/min. This clearly indicates one goal set by a major paper machine producer for their products.

Other printing paper grades have followed the width and speed development of newsprint closely.

Another measure of technical development is water consumption in the production of pulp and paper shown in Table 4.

Table 4. Water consumption in pulp and paper production since 1970.

	1970 m^3/t	1980 m^3/t	1990 m^3/t	1995 m^3/t
Pulp	120	80	30	15
Paper	80	50	20	10

The lowest figure for pulp is the estimated consumption at the Rauma pulp mill in Finland – spring 1996 startup – when normal production levels have been achieved.

In effluent level, both biological oxygen demand (BOD) and suspended solid levels have decreased from 1980 to 1995 by approximately 90–95% per ton of production. New technologies allow reuse of waste water in the process. This further diminishes fresh water demand and brings pulp and paper mills one step closer to being an effluent free, closed loop pulp and paper production system.

A final fact is the dramatic increase in the use of recovered paper in the last 10–15 years. In Europe, the amount of recovered paper used as a raw material has increased from approximately 30% in 1980 to 42% of total fiber consumption in 1995. Because fillers and other additives have also increased their levels from 7% to 13%, wood pulp amount has declined from more than 60% to less than 45% in 1995[2]. This development would not have been possible without dramatic developments in deinking technology and paper machine wet-end chemistry.

Main characteristics of the global forest industry

2.3 Concentration

Global concentration of the forest industry has increased significantly. In Europe, the development has been particularly dramatic. The top ten companies have increased their share of total sales from less than 30% in 1980 to approximately 50% in 1995. In the United States, this development has been much less dramatic during the above period because a 50% concentration level already existed from the early 1980s.

Another measure of concentration is the ownership across borders within the 12 European Union countries. This has increased from 22% in 1976 to 45% in 1994[1]. Major examples of acquisitions that have led to concentration and ownership across borders have been KNP-Leykam, Stora-Feldmühle-Beghin, SCA-Reed-Laakirchen-PWA, UPM-Kymmene-Chapelle Darblay, Enso-Berghuizer-Holtzmann, Norske Skog-KNP Bruck, Metsä-Serla-MD Papier-Biberist, etc.

2.4 Cyclical nature of the forest industry

The forest industry is a cyclical industry. The main reason is the fluctuation of prices for end products – sawn goods, market pulp, newsprint, fine papers, board grades etc. Figure 2 shows the real price of Northern Bleached Softwood Kraft Pulp (NBSKP) in 1950–2000.

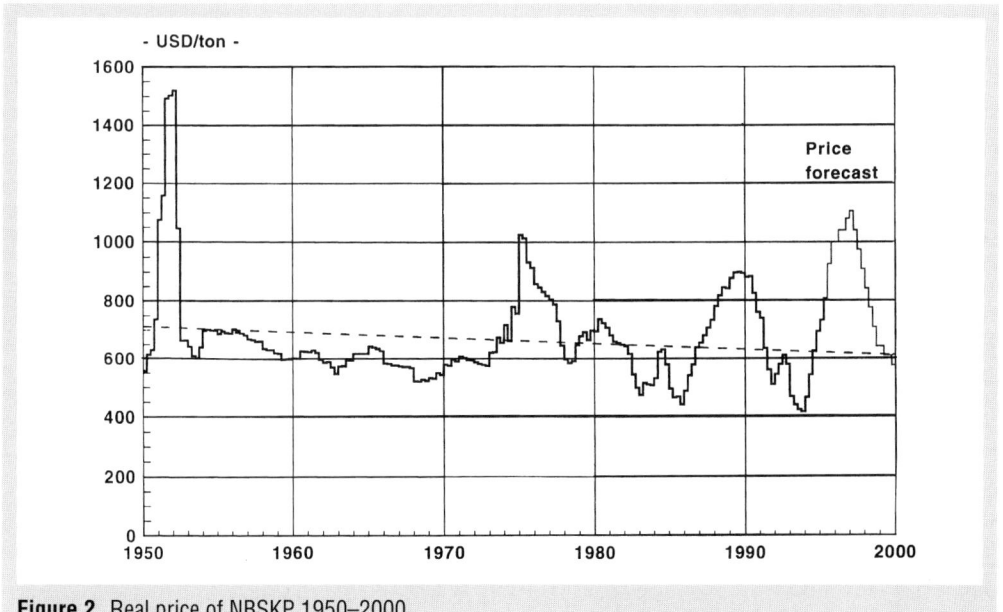

Figure 2. Real price of NBSKP 1950–2000.

The profit figures of North American and European companies reflect the cyclical nature of the forest industry.

CHAPTER 1

The reasons for the cyclical nature of forest industry product prices have undergone discussion, analysis, and debate at great length. The main reasons seem to be the following:
1. Volatility in the demand and supply balance: the result of simultaneous new investment decisions causes supply to increase rapidly, at a faster rate than the demand.
2. Inventory speculation by customers: during expected increasing price cycles, customers purchase more than end users demand. This strengthens the demand and increases the price trend even further. During declining price trends, this mechanism is reversed, thus lowering the demand and strengthening the declining price trend.

Based on these factors, the forest industry and its customers both obviously contribute to the cyclical nature of the industry. Economic fluctuations are also a factor, but of lesser magnitude. Some major banks have tried to establish a futures market for certain forest products such as market pulp in 1996 and 1997. Success has been limited to date. This would seem to indicate that the cyclical nature of the forest industry will continue in the foreseeable future.

2.5 High investment rates

The pulp and paper industry has a characteristic high level of investment rates, causing the industry to be capital intensive. The fact that the capital turnover by most companies is below 1 accentuates this. In the case of investment in new facilities such as pulp and paper mills, the capital turnover is 0.3–0.5 as Table 5 shows for the middle 1990s.

Table 5. Capital turnover of new pulp and newsprint mills at full production.

	Capacity t/a	Investment MFIM	Sales at full production MFIM	Capital turnover
New pulp mill	550 000	2 800	1 350	0.48
New newsprint mill	280 000	2 500	1 000	0.40

The main reasons for high investment rates have been the following:
1. The market growth in many paper grades has been rapid at 4–8% per year. This has forced companies that have wanted to maintain or increase their market shares in these rapidly growing grades to invest heavily in order to maintain their position.
2. As indicated in section 1.2.2. on technical development, technical progress in the pulp and paper industry has been fast. This has given new, well designed mills and machines a competitive advantage in terms of manufacturing costs and quality. This has also motivated investments in some instances.

The average fixed investment level in Europe and North America since 1980 has varied as Figure 3 shows[2].

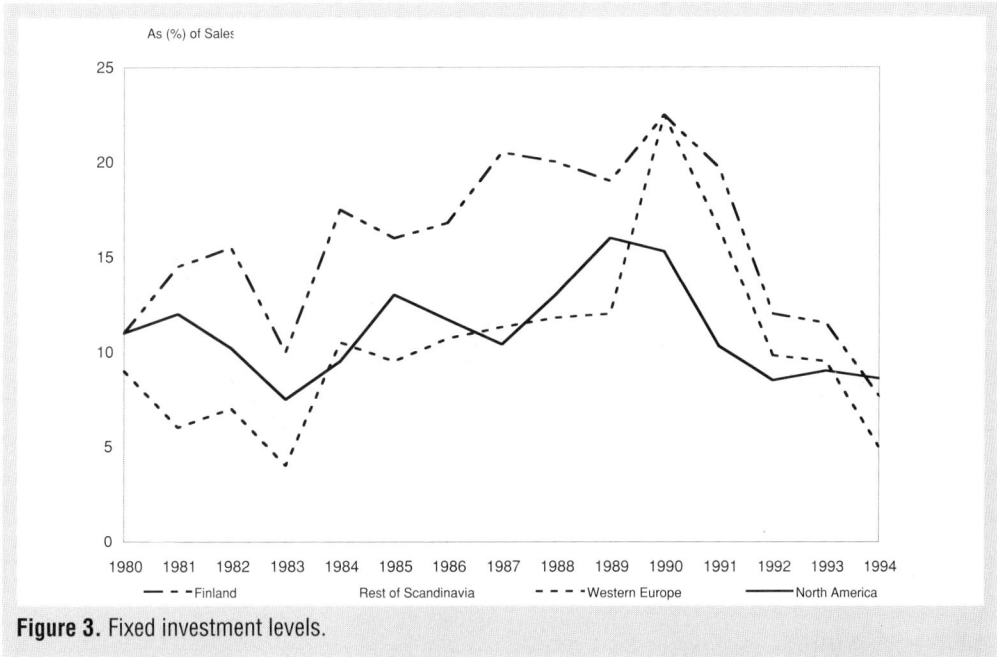

Figure 3. Fixed investment levels.

The above figure illustrates the cyclical nature of the investments that has contributed to the cyclical nature of output, product prices, and profitability discussed also in section 1.2.4.

3 Opportunities for the forest industry

Paper has certain inherited characteristics. Although much debated and not always clearly agreed upon, these characteristics govern its success as a product. They will contribute to its growing demand for many years in the future. Following are the characteristics:
1. Paper uses a renewable raw material – trees.
2. Pulp and paper contribute to the growth of forests, which reduce the carbon dioxide (CO_2) content of the atmosphere and also reduce the greenhouse effect.
3. Paper can be recycled several times, according to some experts 5–7 times. This reduces the need for waste disposal, since used paper returns to the manufacturing cycle.
4. Modern pulp and paper manufacturing processes are so energy efficient that the production of fine paper integrated with pulp manufacture does not require outside energy.

CHAPTER 1

Using these facts, one can ask whether any other industrial product exists, that uses a renewable resource, without outside energy and can be recycled 5–7 times? The answer to this question lays a solid foundation on which the paper industry can thrive and develop in the future.

Another positive aspect for paper is its growth potential. According to Jaakko Pöyry Consulting Oy, global paper consumption is estimated to grow from 260 million tons in 1995 to 400 million tons in 2010. This corresponds to an annual growth of 2.9% per year. Demand should be particularly strong in Asia and the Pacific Rim countries where population and industrial growth will both be strong. The number of people in Asia and the Pacific Rim countries having a GDP in excess of USD 6000 per capita will increase from 400 million in 1995 to 1 000 million in 2010. This is 6.3% per year[3, 4]. The consumption of paper in these households will increase enormously owing to their newly acquired purchasing power. This will contribute to a growth unknown in Europe and North America.

Further development in paper quality through resource reduction, better printability properties, more recycling, closed loop effluent free mills, etc., are all areas where progress can be made to improve further the competitiveness of paper and safeguard its future as a respected and usable industrial product.

4 Threats to the forest industry

In 1996, the paper industry faced the following main threats:
1. The poor image of the industry as an old, smokestack industry with high environmental emissions in air, water and soil.
2. The public belief that the forest industry is responsible for cutting rain forests and old northern forests, monoculture cultivation when planting new trees, excessive clear cutting in sensitive forest areas, etc.
3. Decrease in demand of printing and writing papers, particularly newsprint due to new media.

The following discussion highlights some aspects of the above issues:
1. The environmental consciousness of the industry began to emerge during the early 1970s due to the fact that mill sizes and numbers in combination with increasing production volumes started to affect the environment negatively. Legislation increased also. During the 1980s, both environmental technology and investments in antipollution measures increased significantly. This trend still continues. On an aggregate level, the total environmental load, despite large production, is obviously decreasing and will continue to do so in the future.
Further pressure in these matters began at the end of the 1980s and during the 1990s by environmental groups such as Greenpeace, World Wildlife Fund (WWF), etc. While the arguments and methods used by these groups have not always been substantially correct, they have made a positive contribution

Main characteristics of the global forest industry

in improving the awareness of environmental aspects in public opinion and in the industry.

Early in 1996, the environmental pollution of the industry as an issue appeared to be gradually fading as the industry as a whole reduced environmental emissions to levels of minimal concern.

2. Forest utilization

Forestry and forest use have become subjects of considerable focus by the public, environmentalists, consumers and industry in the mid 1990s. One problem related to these issues is the fact that they are very difficult or almost impossible to define quantitatively. Therefore the main arguments in these discussions are qualitative aspects and opinions.

A clearly defined, responsible forestry policy is essential to the forest industry in general and each forest company in particular. Essential parts of such a policy must be open information and communication to the public. These have not traditionally been the strong points of the industry.

With some exceptions, those forests used and tended globally by the forest industry are in good or at least acceptable condition. The exceptions to this are certain forest companies in Asia and the Pacific Rim that use rain forests as a source of raw material. Past practices in Canada also do not meet the level of responsible forest use. It should be noted that forests in overpopulated areas with no forest industry are often in the greatest danger of permanent damage.

To improve its image in forest and forestry issues, the industry faces a number of challenges. If these questions are not resolved, the image of the industry and its methods of securing sources of raw material for production will be in question. This would put the future of the whole industry in grave jeopardy.

3. Importance of electronic media and technology

The impact of the electronic media on printing paper consumption has been a topic of discussion and analysis for many years. Before the mid 1990s, positive, demand increasing factors have been dominant. Copying technology has been the driving force of printing and copying paper (A4) consumption. Demand in Europe has increased from 0.84 million tons in 1980 to 2.13 million tons in 1995 – 6.4% per year. Personal computers have created a huge demand for user manuals, magazines etc. All these increase the demand for paper. While these developments have been positive, electronic devices have also partially or totally replaced certain paper grades. As an example, computer memories replaced punch cards in the 1960s. Copying machines have almost totally replaced carbon paper. The rapid growth of OTC (single-use carbon) papers in the 1970s and early 1980s has turned to a decline.

In the United States, there are signs in the mid 1990s that the growth of newsprint demand has stopped and possibly started to decline. Television, the Internet, and other electronic media are suspected reasons. Certain large newsprint producers such as Stora in Sweden have decided not to increase

CHAPTER 1

their newsprint production any more due to low or negative demand prospects[5].

A favorable factor for the continuing global growth of newsprint demand is the increasing number of affluent, middle-aged or elderly people in the highly populated Asia and Pacific Rim region who are unaccustomed to computers. In principle, this statement applies to Europe and North America also. However, electronic media is a growing competitor to printing papers and might cause a slowing or even a decline of demand for these grades within the next 5–10 years.

Sources

1. CEPI (Confederation of European Paper Industries)
2. Jaakko Pöyry Consulting Oy
3. World Bank
4. Pac Rim
5. Stora Annual Report 1995

CHAPTER 2

Impact of the forest industry on the economy of Finland

1	General	21
2	Historical and present production	21
3	Exports	22
4	Forest increment and drain	24
5	Labor force and productivity	25
6	Investments	26
7	Comparison to other countries	27
	Sources	28

CHAPTER 2

Impact of the forest industry on the economy of Finland

1 General

The Finnish economy is based on the forest industry, more than that of any other country in the world. Finland has been able to use one of its few natural resources to build a national economy and standard of living that rank among the highest in the world. GDP per capita in 1995 was USD 17 200 for a ranking of 18 among Organization for Economic Co-operation and Development (OECD) countries. This was approximately 35% lower than the GDP per capita of the United States, the world leader with USD 26 500 GDP per capita[1].

2 Historical and present production

The Finnish forest industry started its development at the end of the eighteenth century. Two new inventions – the groundwood and sulfite processes – were applied on an industrial scale utilising spruce, which grew in Finland. Sawmilling completed and contributed to the growth of the forest sector.

Table 1 shows the production volumes of main forest products[2].

Table 1. Development of forest industry production in Finland 1960–1995.

	1960	1970	1980	1990	1995
Sawn goods (1000 m3/a)	7 737	7 310	10 230	7 400	9 500
Pulp (1000 t/a)	3 516	6 233	7 246	8 886	10 088
Paper and board (1000 t/a)	1 970	4 258	5 919	8 966	10 942

CHAPTER 2

Table 2 shows the growth of paper and board production volumes and products since 1960[2].

Table 2. Development of paper and board production in Finland 1960–1995.

	1960 1000 t/a	1970 1000 t/a	1980 1000 t/a	1990 1000 t/a	1995 1000 t/a
Newsprint	774	1 305	1 569	1 429	1 425
Mechanical printing and writing paper	146	753	1 577	3 333	4 385
Fine papers	88	171	450	1 349	1 929
Tissue	0	100	137	171	0[1]
Liner and fluting			614	708	0[1]
Boxboard	962[2]	1 929[2]	600	918	1 298
Others			972	1 058	1 905[1]
Total	1 970	4 258	5 919	8 966	10 942

[1] including tissue, liner and fluting
[2] incl. liner & fluting, boxboard and others in 1960 & 1970

The data indicates two main growth sectors – printing and writing papers and fine papers – where growth has clearly exceeded the average. Newsprint production has remained stable since 1970.

3 Exports

Exporting has been and still remains today the major part of the forest industry's production in Finland. Imports of any forest product to Finland are negligible compared with exports. Table 3 presents the development of exports since 1960[2]:

Table 3. Export volumes of Finnish forest products 1960–1995.

	1960	1970	1980	1990	1995
Sawn goods (1000 m³/a)	5 339	4 702	6 939	4 173	7 000
Market pulp (1000 t/a)	1 594	2 057	1 939	1 461	1 320
Paper and board (1000 t/a)	1 610	3 522	4 792	7 699	9 630

The share of forest products in the total exports has developed as Table 4 shows[2].

Table 4. Export value of Finnish forest products 1960–1995.

	1960	1970	1980	1990	1995
Sawn goods (MFIM)	824	924	4 960	4 900	7 280
Market pulp (MFIM)	509	1 205	3 414	3 673	4 400
Paper and board (MFIM)	763	2 314	10 039	24 877	39 100
Total forest products (MFIM)[1]	2 176	5 289	22 397	38 142	59 000
Total exports from Finland (MFIM)	3 165	9 687	52 973	101 339	174 660
Share of forest products (%)	69	55	42	38	34

[1] incl. others

These tables indicate that the share of forest industry exports of the total exports has declined from 69% in 1960 to 34% in 1995. During the last five years, the relative share has stabilized due to a strong increase in production volumes of the forest industry and to difficulties in increasing exports in other fields.

The share of forest products of the total exports, although in a declining trend, is still significant. Many other product groups such as forest industry automatization and electronic equipment, pulp and paper machinery, machinery in forest operation, consulting, etc., use the knowhow developed in cooperation with the forest industry. The value of these cluster products adds to the share of forest industry exports and to the GDP and total standard of living.

The above consideration gains in significance when using net export value as a measurement. (Net export value is the value of export minus that of imports.) Most forest industry products need a small amount of imported products in the manufacturing process as Table 5 shows.

Table 5. Estimated sales value share of imported materials in Finnish forest products.

	Sales value	Import input	Net export value
Sawn goods	100	~1	~99
Pulp	100	3-20[1]	80-97[1]
Newsprint	100	~1	~99
Printing and writing papers	100	~10	~90
Fine papers	100	~10	~90
Boxboards	100	~10	~90

[1] depending on input of imported wood

CHAPTER 2

For exports of many engineering products such as paper machines, the input of imports is significantly higher – approximately 35%.

The above figures show that roughly 60% of Finnish net export value comes from the products manufactured by the forest industry. This figure does not include any forest industry cluster products.

4 Forest increment and drain

Forest increment or growth and total drain or total wood consumption including natural drain in Finland has developed as Table 6 shows[2].

Table 6. Forest increment and total drain in Finland 1960–1995.

	1960 million m^3	1970 million m^3	1980 million m^3	1990 million m^3	1995 million m^3
Increment	56	57	67	81	84
Total drain	61	57	60	55	60

The increment has exceeded drain in all years except some during the 1960s. During the end of the 1980s and during the 1990s, the gap between the increment and drain widened.

Table 7 gives the wood supply sources in the mid 1990s[2]:

Table 7. Wood supply sources in 1995.

	1995 million m^3
Private forest owners	39
Industry owned forests	4
State and municipalities	7
Imports	11[1)
Exports	-1
Total	60

1) normal import level is 7-8 million m^3/a

Using the facts in Table 6, one could argue that due to excess wood growth in comparison to demand forest industry capacity could expand considering the availability of domestic raw material. This conclusion seems valid particularly if the level of wood imports remains at the high level of 1995. Several factors speak against the availability of domestic wood for increased expansion:

1. Wood consumption will increase from the 1995 level by approximately 15% owing to capacity expansions already decided such as Kaukopää CTMP-start, Rauma Light Weight Coated (LWC) machine, Kaukas pulp, Metsä-Rauma pulp mill and Kirkniemi LWC machine.

2. Concern about forestry and forest protection is increasing. Protected forest areas that cannot be used as a source of raw material will increase from the present 3.2 million hectares (ha).
3. Many forest owners are not as dependent on income from forest cuttings as earlier. The will to harvest has therefore declined. Taxation of forest income adds to the reluctance to cut forests and the notion that forest growth gives better returns in the long term than on today's cuttings.

In practice and reality, wood availability in 1994 during the strong demand for many forest products was critical and raised concern about secured wood supply without excess price increases. The accepted opinion in the forest industry is that significant expansion of capacity based on additional wood removals will no longer be possible after the mid 1990s. New production should therefore use present market pulp only for higher value-added products such as paper. If this opinion is correct, future investments must expand abroad to a greater extent than earlier, if the forest industry is to maintain its global market share. This will be a significant change for both the Finnish forest industry and the national economy of Finland. The country will slowly lose one of its key economic driving forces.

5 Labor force and productivity

Table 8 shows development of the direct labor force of the forest industry[2].

Table 8. Labor force 1980–1995.

	1980 1000 persons	1995 1000 persons	Change %/a
Paper industry	45	28	-2.0
Mechanical forest industry	30	12	-3.8
Forestry and floating	14	5	-4.2
Salaried employees	20	15	-1.2
Total	109	60	-2.5

In 1994, the total labor force in Finland was 3.8 million[1]. The direct share of the forest industry was therefore less than 2% and declining according to the figures in the table.

The productivity calculated per labor unit has increased dramatically. Pulp and paper production in 1980 was 13.2 million tons. In 1995, the corresponding figure was 21.0 million tons. If the productivity index per labor unit in 1980 was 100, it was 250 in 1995. This corresponds to an annual increase of 6.3%.

CHAPTER 2

6 Investments

Total domestic investments of the forest industry in Finland since 1980 have developed as Table 9 shows[2].

Table 9. Domestic investments of the Finnish forest industry 1980–1995.

	Domestic investments billion FIM	Domestic investments/sales %
1980	2.7	10
1981	3.3	11
1982	3.4	12
1983	2.8	9
1984	3.2	8
1985	4.1	10
1986	4.0	10
1987	5.2	12
1988	6.1	12
1989	8.5	16
1990	8.2	16
1991	6.2	14
1992	6.0	12
1993	3.2	6.2
1994	5.0	8.0
1995	8.5	11.2
Total	80.4	
Annual average	5.0	11.1

The figures in the Table 9 lead to the following conclusions:
1. During 1980–1996, the total investment value has been 80 billion FIM or 5.0 billion FIM per year. This equals an average investment rate of 11.1% of sales.
2. The share of the mechanical forest industry out of the total 80 billion FIM has been approximately 15%.
3. The highest relative investment rate occurred in 1989–1990 approximately 16% of sales. The lowest rate during this period was approximately 6% of sales in 1993.
4. The share of forest industry investments in total industrial investments excluding power, gas, and water supply was 36% in 1980–1996[1]. The forest industry is therefore a strong driving force in the Finnish economy. This figure would be even higher if the cluster effect was included.

7 Comparison to other countries

The impact of the forest industry on the national economy is larger in Finland than in any other country in the world as Table 10 shows[2].

Table 10. Forest industry share of total national exports.

	Forest industry % of total national exports	Forest industry exports FIM per capita
Finland	34	10 393
Sweden	19	6 067
Canada	14	4 229
U.S.A.	4	372
Austria	10	2 990
Norway	4	1 824

Any fluctuation and the cyclical nature of the forest industry income in Finland can have more serious consequences there than in other countries.

CHAPTER 2

Sources

1. The Research Institute of the Finnish Economy (ETLA)
2. Finnish Forest Industry Federation

CHAPTER 3

Raw material resources – wood supply

1	**Introduction**	**30**
2	**Wood costs – definitions**	**31**
3	**Wood supply**	**32**
3.1	General	32
3.2	Finland	33
3.3	Sweden	37
3.4	Europe excluding Scandinavia	41
3.5	Canada	42
3.6	United States	43
3.7	South America	44
3.8	Other areas	45
	Sources	46

CHAPTER 3

Raw material resources – wood supply

1 Introduction

The total raw material supply needed by the forest industry in the mid 1990s is approximately 320 million tons from the sources in Table 1.

Table 1. Raw materials.

	%	Million tons
1. Wood based raw materials	55	176
2. Recycled fiber	30	96
3. Minerals and chemicals	12	38
4. Non-wood fiber	3	10
	100 %	**320**

The use of recycled fiber has increased considerably from approximately 20% of the total furnish composition in 1970 to 30% 25 years later. The share may increase to 40% by 2010[2].

The forest industry has traditionally been located near raw material resources. In North America and Scandinavia, this generally meant close to forests. The increasing use of recycled fiber has caused building new mills near recycled fiber sources. These are densely populated areas with high standards of living and high paper consumption per capita.

Depending on the paper grade produced, the availability and price of wood raw material or recycled fiber are key success factors. Often they are primary success factors. This is due to the large share of manufacturing costs represented by fiber in most paper grades.

Table 2. Fiber cost share of manufacturing costs of major forest products in 1995.

	fiber costs share of manufacturing costs [1]
Sawn goods	65
Chemical pulp	65
Newsprint (recycled)	45
LWC	16

[1] Manufacturing costs = total costs excl. capital costs

Table 2 illustrates the significance of fiber costs in certain forest product grades in 1995.

The share of fiber costs in lower value products is high. Particularly in these goods, low unit fiber costs are necessary for successful operation. In higher value products such as light weight coated (LWC) grades, the influence of wood costs is much lower and of less importance.

During the 1990s, a growing concern emerged concerning wood supply. Forest devastation, loss of biodiversity in natural forests, loss of habitats for animal and plant species, etc., resulted in restrictions on the use of natural forests for logging and silviculture. A negative attitude toward fast-growing plantations also increased. Partly due to these facts, a fiber scarcity in certain traditional supply areas, such as the Pacific North American region emerged. A secured fiber supply with reasonable cost and value assumes increasing importance for the forest industry on the eve of the third millennium.

2 Wood costs – definitions

1. Measurement of wood
   This book uses the following definitions for measuring wood:
   - m^3 sub = m^3 solid under bark (excludes bark and top of tree)
   - m^3 sob = m^3 solid over bark (includes bark and top of tree).
2. Costs of wood
   Wood costs at a mill consist of stumpage, harvesting, transport, and administrative costs. Stumpage costs cover all costs necessary to grow the trees including profit and taxes. In countries with private forests, the forest owner receives stumpage payment. In Canada, stumpage payment goes to the province as concession rights.
   Harvesting cost includes cutting, removing branches, and transport to roadside for storing and further transport. The transport distance to roadside is normally less than 500 m.
   Transport costs include transport from roadside to mill with loading and unloading.
   Administrative costs include the costs for the organization covering the wood procurement.

In Finland, the components of wood costs excluding administrative costs in 1995 were as follows:

Stumpage	66%
Harvesting	21%
Transport	13%
Total	100%

Note that comparisons of wood costs between different regions are very difficult. Exchange rate variations, different volume measurements, differences in wood densities, etc., add to the inaccuracies inherent in any comparison.

3 Wood supply

3.1 General

The total forest area of the world in tropical and nontropical zones was approximately 3.5 billion ha in 1990[1]. Table 3 summarises the data in more detail and also indicates the estimated change since 1980.

Table 3. Estimated global forest area in 1980 and 1990.

	1980 Forest Area million ha	1990 Forest Area million ha	Total Change 1980-1990 million ha	Average annual change %
Tropical areas				
Africa	568.6	527.6	-41.0	-0.7
Asia/Pacific	349.6	310.6	-39.0	-1.2
Latin America/Caribbean	992.2	918.1	-74.1	-0.8
Subtotal tropical	1 910.4	1 756.3	-154.1	-0.8
Non-tropical areas				
Africa	19.2	21.4	+2.2	+1.1
Asia/Pacific	240.5	245.4	+4.9	+0.2
Latin America/Caribbean	90.9	93.7	+2.8	+0.3
North America	464.6	456.7	-7.9	-0.2
Europe	147.8	149.3	+1.5	+0.1
Former Soviet Union	732.4	755.0	+22.6	+0.3
Subtotal non-tropical	1 695.4	1 721.5	+26.1	+0.2
World total	3 605.8	3 477.8	-128.0	-0.4

Sources: Forest Resources Assessment 1980 Tropical Countries, FAO 1993
The Forest Resources of the Temperate Zones, FAO 1993

One can draw the following conclusions from the data:
- In 1990, nontropical forest area grew by 0.2% per year. The tropical forest area decreased by 0.8% or 15 million ha per year. This trend is likely to continue and is a reason for great concern.

Raw material resources – wood supply

- The above forest area supplied the global need for wood that was estimated at 3.5 billion m³ in 1990. One estimate states that 54% of this was used for fuel, 33% was for industrial purposes such as saw logs and construction boards, and the remaining 13% was for the pulp and paper industry. Developing countries consume 80% of the fuel wood.
- Based on the Food and Agriculture Organization of the United Nations (FAO) estimates in Table 4, wood consumption will increase to 4.1 billion m³ by the year 2000 and 4.7 billion m³ in 2010 because of global population increase[1]. At the same time, the forest area will decrease to 3.3 and 3.1 billion ha, respectively.

Table 4. Population, forests, and wood consumption in 2010[1].

	1980	1990	2000	2010
Population	4.44	5.28	6.18	7.03
Forest area (ha)	3.61	3.44	3.25*	3.06*
Wood consumption (bill. m³)	2.93	3.51	4.09*	4.66

* = estimate
Sources: FAO Forest Resources Assessment 1990, Global Synthesis (1995)

The forest industry must ensure that the forest resources of the world are not depleted. A vital, flourishing industry requires a vital, flourishing forest to survive. The fiber production of the forest industry in the mid 1990s used 80% virgin fiber. This came from 30% natural, managed regeneration, 23% from plantations, 14% from unmanaged natural regeneration, and 14% from original forests[2]. In the future, the two first categories must increase, and the final two must decrease.

The role of forest plantation is evolving. Theoretically, 40 million ha of high-yield industrial plantations could fill the global fiber need. This is less than 1.5% of the total global forest area. Although theoretical, this example shows that the combination of managed natural forests and high-yield plantations is the key to successful long-term forest management.

3.2 Finland

Finland's total productive forest area is 20 million ha[3]. The average growing stock of the Finnish forests is 95 m³/ha. Six million ha of unproductive areas also resemble forests. They have a few trees per hectare with slow or no growth. These areas are not productive forest areas and are not part of the 20 million ha above.

Since forests constitute an important natural resource of the country, forestry research, legislation, and management receive high priority. Forest inventory audits are continuous. The country is divided into 14 districts. Two districts receive a thorough inventory every year. This data replaces the old data so the oldest information dates from an inventory seven years earlier.

CHAPTER 3

Typical characteristics of Finnish forests are slow growth due to climactic conditions, high utilization rate – usage/growth – and a limited number of wood species.
Figure 1 shows the forest balance in Finland for 1960–1994[3].

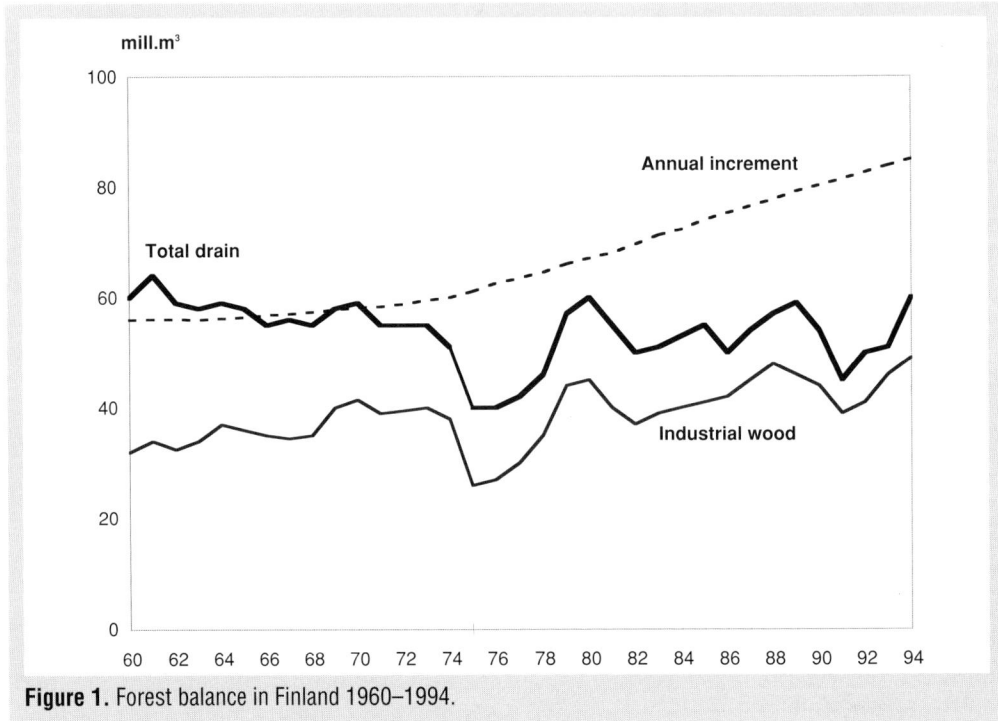

Figure 1. Forest balance in Finland 1960–1994.

The data leads to the following conclusions:
1. Industrial wood consumption of domestic origin has grown from 32 million m^3 in 1960 to 50 million m^3 in the mid 1990s.
2. Total drain of wood has been 40–60 million m^3 per year since 1960. The trend was declining from 1960 to 1975. From 1975, the trend has increased without, however, reaching the peak figures of the early 1960s.
3. The difference between total drain and industrial usage consists mostly of other uses such as wood for fuel, sawmill residues, natural drain, etc. This has declined from approximately 30 million m^3 in 1960 to approximately 10 million m^3 per year at the present time.
4. Total drain has been lower than the annual increment with the exception of 1960–1964 when the balance was negative by approximately 4 million m^3.
5. The annual increment has grown steadily from 1965 and has reached 85 million m^3 per year in the middle 1990s. This leads to the conclusion that there is a growing amount of unused wood since the total annual drain by the middle 1990s was approximately 60 million m^3.

Raw material resources – wood supply

Table 5. Ownership structure of Finnish forests.

	Forest land area %	Standing stock %	Growth %
Private	62	70	73
Industry	9	8	10
State of Finland	24	17	12
Municipal, others	5	5	5
Total	100	100	100

Table 5 shows the high percentage of private forest owners. The average forest holding in this category is 10 ha[3]. This results in 100 000 wood purchase agreements annually between the private forest owners and the industry.

An area of 3.2 million ha of the total Finnish forest – productive and unproductive – is protected.

Wood supply sources

Table 7 in Chapter 2 shows the wood supply sources in 1995. One of the conclusions is that private forest owners hold a key position as suppliers. This is to be expected considering their large ownership share of the total forest area in Finland.

The small share of industry-owned forests indicates that the industry cannot control or dictate wood prices.

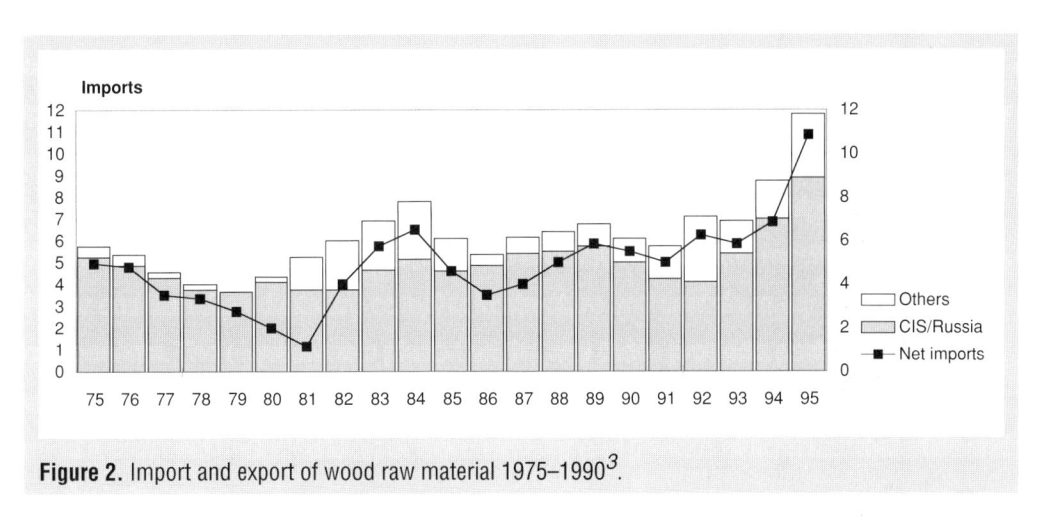

Figure 2. Import and export of wood raw material 1975–1990[3].

CHAPTER 3

Imports form an essential part of the wood supply. The major part of the imported wood comes from Western Russia as birch – (9.0 million m^3 in 1995 in a total of 12.0 million m^3). Since the Russian forest industry does not have industrial uses for birch, the exports provide work for local people and generate much needed export revenues for the local economy.

Figure 2 shows that wood import trends have been growing since the early 1980s from 4 million m^3 per year to 12 million m^3 in the mid 1990s. During the same period, exports have declined from nearly 3 million m^3 to 1 million m^3 per year.

Wood costs

Figure 3 shows the development of average wood costs for all species and grades since 1985[3].

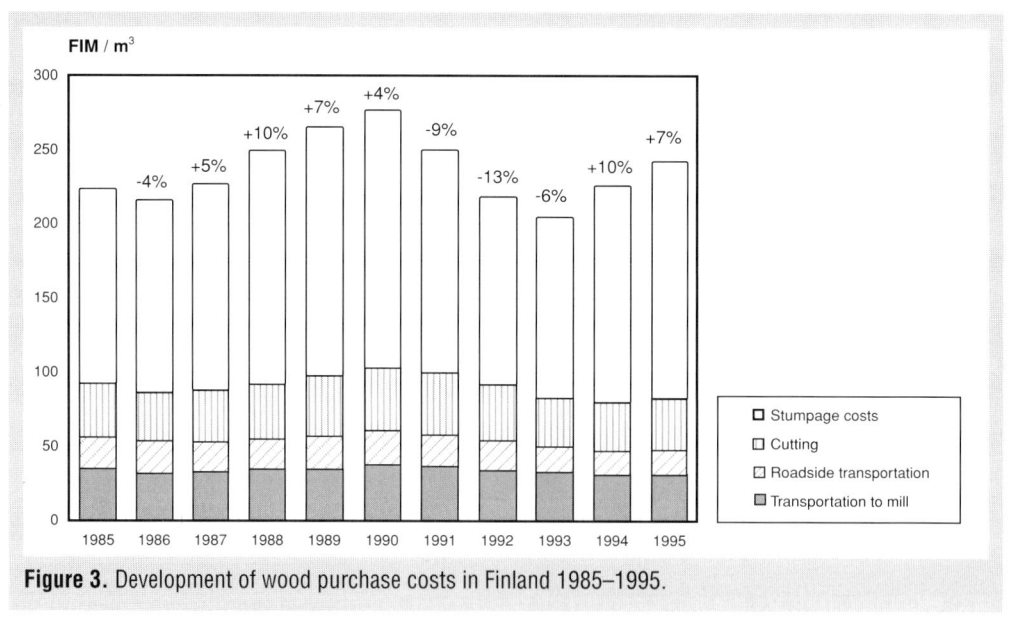

Figure 3. Development of wood purchase costs in Finland 1985–1995.

The following conclusions can be made:
1. Stumpage forms approximately 65% of total wood costs at the mill. The remaining part is divided between cutting and logging at approximately 20% and transport from roadside to mill at 15%.
2. Nominal wood costs in 1985–1995 have fluctuated, but the average has remained constant.

Future outlook

Wood consumption – total drain – cannot increase much above the level achieved at the end of the 1990s. This is approximately 65 million m^3 per year. Although annual growth exceeds this amount, the risks of increasing the utilization rate of forests are likely to prevent further expansion. The following are the main risks involved:

1. Economy of scale has increased the size of modern pulp and paper mills to such an extent that the high raw material volume must come from larger areas. This increases transportation distances especially in Finland where wood usage rate everywhere is already at a high level. This increases wood transportation costs and wood costs at a mill.
2. Importing wood to Finland is a structured risk and weakness accentuated by certification requirements and the economic and political instability of the supplying countries. Since lower wood imports require a higher domestic wood supply, the present positive wood balance is a reserve for any curtailment of imports.
3. It is probable that the protected forest areas in Finland will expand to reduce wood availability for industrial use compared to the present level.
4. The private forest owners who were traditionally farmers have increasingly changed to become part of the urban population. Their dependence on forest income is considerably smaller, and their interest in tending their forest holdings has declined. Their willingness to sell has also declined. Taxation of forest income has had an important influence on their willingness and desire to sell. The taxation of forest income used forest growth rather than actual income from wood sales until the 1990s. This was a positive factor to increase the willingness of forest owners to sell. The changes in the taxation laws gave the forest owners a choice between continuing the old method using growth or a new method using sales income of wood. It has become apparent that the new taxation method will not increase willingness to sell but the opposite.

3.3 Sweden

The total forest area in Sweden is 23.2 million ha with an average growing stock per hectare of 112 m^3. The Swedish and Finnish forests are very similar except that climactic conditions make the growth in Swedish forests slightly higher.

CHAPTER 3

Increment, drain and ownership structure

Table 6 shows the increment and drain of wood in Swedish forests for 1960–1995[4].

Table 6. Annual growth and total drain in Sweden 1960–1995

	Total drain million m³fub	Annual increment million m³
1960	55.8	83
1961	58.3	82
1962	54.6	82
1963	62.6	81
1964	62.6	80
1965	61.6	80
1966	69.0	79
1967	60.5	78
1968	65.3	78
1969	74.1	77
1970	80.0	80
1971	71.1	82
1972	73.7	81
1973	76.3	82
1974	69.5	82
1975	66.7	84
1976	56.0	88
1977	56.6	89
1978	57.2	92
1979	58.2	94
1980	60.8	97
1981	61.6	99
1982	65.4	100
1983	65.3	96
1984	63.0	98
1985	63.1	96
1986	64.4	101
1987	65.5	101
1988	67.5	100
1989	65.6	102
1990	64.0	99
1991	66.3	
1992	67.2	
1993	70.3	
1994	72.8	
1995	68.0 est.	

Source: Riksskogstaxeringen, Skogsstyrelsen

Raw material resources – wood supply

The following conclusions can be drawn:
1. Annual increment has grown from approximately 80 million m³ in the late 1950s and 1960s to approximately 100 million m³ per year in the early 1990s.
2. The total drain of wood has grown from nearly 55 million m³ per year to approximately 70 million m³ per year during the same period. The annual increment has therefore exceeded total drain every year since 1960. The age structure of Swedish forests compared with Finland must be older and the wood density by area higher.

Table 7 shows the ownership structure of Swedish forests[4].

Table 7. Ownership structure of Swedish forests.

	Forest land area %
Private	50
Industry	38
State of Sweden	4
Municipal, others	8
Total	100

In the early 1990s, private forest owners had approximately 245 000 forest lots. The average size per forest lot was then approximately 48 ha. Of the total area of productive Swedish forests, approximately 760 000 ha or 3.3% have protection from use for industrial purposes.

Supply sources of wood

Table 8 shows the supply of wood for 1992–1994[4].

Table 8. Wood supply sources 1992–1994 (3 year average).

	Million m³
Private	40.6
Industry, state, others	27.2
Total	67.8

Assuming that industry, state and other forest owners supplied an equal amount in proportion to land area, industry supplied 21 million m³. The state and other owners supplied the remaining 6 million m³. In comparison to Finland, the Swedish forest industry owns a significantly larger forest area. Table 9 shows the largest industrial forest owners.

CHAPTER 3

Table 9. Largest industrial forest owners in Sweden 1995.

	Forest land area 1 000 ha
Stora	2 300
SCA	1 800
MoDo	1 040
ASSI	3 350
Total	8 490

These forest holdings should improve the operating margins and cash flow of the above companies compared with Finnish companies.

Industry forest holdings combined with the positive wood supply and demand balance should maintain wood prices in Table 10[4].

Table 10. Pulp wood prices 1984/85–1994/95.

	1984/1985 SEK / m^3	1989/1990 SEK / m^3	1994/95 SEK / m^3
Pine	209	279	253
Spruce	225	293	278
Birch	180	263	266
All	213	284	267

[1] price delivered at roadside excl. transport to mill

The price increase for all grades from 1984/85 to 1994/95 was 25% or 2.3% per year.

Imports of wood were 4.3 million m^3 in 1980, 4.7 million m^3 in 1990, and 9 million m^3 in 1995. This increasing trend was particularly obvious during the 1990s.

Future outlook

These statistics on the growth and consumption of wood indicate the potential to increase the use of Swedish forests and the domestic production capacity. The forest growth potential does not control the production capacity of the forest industry as in Finland. The development of imports indicates that the forest industry does not obtain all its needs from domestic sources. The reasons for this are similar to the reasons for Finland with particular importance on the following factors:

1. Sweden taxes income from wood sales as an addition to normal income. The resulting high taxation rate – often over 50% – has decreased the interest in cutting and supplying wood.
2. The Swedish forest industry has been more active in overseas investments. This has lessened the need for domestic wood supplies.

3. The availability of recycled fiber has been significantly higher in Sweden than in other Scandinavian countries due to a larger population and higher paper consumption per capita. Importing waste paper from central Europe has been easier due to shorter transport distances especially for southern Sweden. Recycled fiber has therefore replaced wood in many new investment projects.

Despite the potential to increase its capacity using domestic wood, the Swedish forest industry will probably look abroad for new investment opportunities rather than expand strongly at home.

3.4 Europe excluding Scandinavia

The countries with the largest forest regions in Europe are Germany, France, Austria, Spain, Portugal, and England. Table 11 shows their respective forest areas, growth, and wood consumption[2].

Table 11. Forest area, growth, and harvest in certain European countries.

	Land area million ha	Exploitable forest area million ha	Net annual increment mill.m^3/ha	Harvest (1994) mill.m^3/a
Germany	34.9	9.9	58.5	37.0
France	54.3	12.5	65.9	42.9
Austria	8.3	3.3	22.0	15.0
United Kingdom	24.1	2.2	11.1	8.2
Spain	49.9	6.5	27.8	13.8
Portugal	8.7	2.4	11.3	9.8

High average age and growing stock per area are typical for European forests due to low thinning and cutting volumes for a long time. Softwood species are common due to past reforestation practices. This is particularly true for Germany, where almost all forests had been cut by approximately 1850. At the end of the nineteenth century, an active reforestation program began. It used predominantly spruce for economic reasons, although climatic conditions place Germany in the hardwood region.

Areas where wood removal exceeds growth are Spain and Portugal. Active planting of eucalyptus could improve the situation if actively pursued and environmentally acceptable. England has practiced active reforestation since World War I. Sitca spruce is the most widely planted tree due to its suitability for mechanical pulp.

The wood supply in Europe could increase from its present level, but reforestation practices, institutional factors, and environmental concerns are likely to prevent this.

Wood costs in Europe vary from country to country. In general, however, wood costs are high. Pulpwood costs at the mill for softwood are 45–55 USD/m^3 and for hardwood 50–65 USD/m^3.

CHAPTER 3

3.5 Canada

Until the late 1970s, the forest resources in Canada were considered to be practically unlimited. This resulted in a low interest in developing forest practices and collecting reliable data on forest inventories, growth, reforestation, etc. Expansion of the national forest industry was considered secure with a high quality and low cost wood supply.

Early in the 1980s, the situation changed dramatically, and the negligence of reforestation during the past decades suddenly became evident. The Allowable Annual Cut (AAC) defining the maximum drain of wood from a given region using sustained forestry was drastically lowered in most regions.

Provincial governments own most Canadian forests. In British Columbia, the province owns 95% of productive timberland. In the central and eastern parts of Canada, provincial ownership varies between 80 and 90%. Due to the high ownership of forests by the provinces, it is common practice in Canada for the forest industry to acquire concessions to use the timber in a certain region as a raw material for industrial manufacture. The influence of the provincial authorities on forestry, reforestation requirements, etc., has therefore been significant.

Table 12 shows the Canadian forest resources per region.

Table 12. Canadian forest resources by region.

	Land area million ha	Productive commercial forest area million ha	Net allowable cut (1993) mill.m^3/ha	Harvest (1993) mill.m^3/a
Atlantic provinces	50.2	21.1	19.6	15.5
Quebec/Ontario	224.8	94.0	92.7	55.2
Prairies (Alb.,Sask.,Man.)	176.3	50.2	39.3	20.0
British Columbia	93.0	49.1	78.8	78.1
Northwest Territories	377.3	21.1		
TOTAL	921.6	235.5	230.4	168.8

These harvest figures show that British Columbia has large forest resources consisting almost exclusively of softwood (pine). This has led to the establishment of a large sawmilling and chemical pulp producing industry. A typical practice in the sawmilling industry is to use only the high quality, large diameter logs in the forests. Chips from the sawmills have then been the sole raw material source of the pulp mills. Many pulp mills have therefore not built a woodyard but relied on chip deliveries from nearby sawmills.

Spruce dominates the forests in eastern Canada. With large amounts of cheap hydroelectric power, this has resulted in the formation of a large newsprint industry in this part of Canada.

Large forest regions in Canada are remote and practically inaccessible for industrial use. With the new outlook on forest resources, this has lowered the expected harvest in the future especially in British Columbia. Major changes in forest management

3.6 United States

The total forest area of the United States is approximately 200 million ha. Table 13 shows the most important forest regions[2].

Table 13. U.S. forest resources by region.

	Land area million ha	Production commercial forest area million ha	Growth (1991) mill.m3/a	Harvest (1991) mill.m3/a
US North	167.3	63.9	151.7	78.9
US South	216.3	80.7	278.2	253.3
Rocky Mountains	300.4	25.3	61.5	23.4
Pacific Coast	231.9	28.3	120.6	105.9
Total	915.9	198.2	612.0	461.5

The data shows that the southern United States is the largest forest area that is commercially productive. Its forests consist of approximately equal amounts of softwood and hardwood. Wood removals balance growth meaning additional wood supplies are not available without intensified silviculture. In some areas, softwood removals exceed growth. The dominant softwood species – southern pine – is used for lumber, chemical pulp, and also kraftliner manufacture. These industries have grown rapidly in the southern United States.

Wood species suitable for mechanical pulp are not common in these forests. Therefore industrial production of mechanical printing paper or virgin fiber newsprint is rare in the area.

Other important forest regions are in the Pacific northwest, north central, and northeast. Softwood species are dominant at approximately 90% of the Pacific northwest. In the other areas, hardwood is common at 75%. The softwood species in these parts of the United States are suitable for mechanical pulp, and newsprint and mechanical printing paper manufacture are common in these regions.

Environmental considerations such as the protection of the spotted owl's habitat curtailed total wood supply in the early 1990s in the Pacific northwest area. An increase of the production capacity in this part of the country is therefore not possible in the present situation. In the north central and northeast regions, some supply potential based primarily on hardwood still exists.

CHAPTER 3

3.7 South America

South America has the world's largest growing stock of hardwood consisting mainly of tropical forests. Due to economical and environmental reasons, these cannot and should not be used for industrial purposes.

Tropical forests have the following typical features:
- a large variety of different wood species
- low amount of growing stock per area
- inaccessibility due to remote location from industrial infrastructure
- poor soil conditions that make change to planted forests difficult
- poor regeneration (when cut, tropical forests do not grow again due to soil erosion during seasonal rains or other plants such as grasses taking over after removal of trees).

The rebirth of tropical forests after removal is unlikely. Attempts to establish planted forests in former tropical forest areas can be successful if well managed. The failures in this respect have far outnumbered the successful attempts so far.

Considering these facts, any additional wood supply in South America should use planted forests. The countries with the best potential are Brazil, Chile, and Argentina.

Brazil

Almost 90% of the land area of Brazil or 700 million ha is forest land. Only a small portion will be used for industrial purposes. The present planted forest area is approximately 4 million ha of which 60% is hardwood – mainly eucalyptus – and 40% softwood. The estimated growth in these planted forests in 1995 was 32 million m^3 softwood and 20 million m^3 hardwood. Removal amounts to approximately 80% of growth. The growth should increase to over 40 million m^3 per year by 2010 for both softwood and hardwood.

Wood costs in Brazil are low. Pulpwood costs at the mill for softwood were approximately USD 35/m^3 and for hardwood were approximately USD 25/m^3 in 1995.

Chile

Chile has approx. 1.5 million hectares of planted forests of which 80% is softwood – Pinus Radiata. The estimated growth in these forests in 1995 was 13 million m^3 of softwood and 4 million m^3 hardwood. Wood costs in Chile are probably the lowest in the world for softwood. In 1995, pulpwood costs at the mill for softwood were approximately USD 25/m^3.

Argentina

There are approximately 0.8 million ha of planted forests in Argentina divided equally as softwood and hardwood. The estimated growth in 1995 was 8 million m^3 softwood and 8 million m^3 hardwood. Removals amount to approximately half the growth. The growth should increase 50% by 2010. Wood costs are at the same level as in Brazil.

3.8 Other areas

Significant forest areas that supply and consume wood for industrial purposes exist besides those mentioned above. The following is a short overview:

- Russia owns half the total world growing stock, an estimated 650 million ha of forest. The majority of these forest areas are presently inaccessible.
- The Baltic states offer a significant growth potential if they intensify forest management practices.
- Australia and New Zealand can increase removals using existing plantations.
- Japan's forests of 24 million ha will increase their growth from the current 55 million m^3 per year by 15 million m^3 per year before 2000. However, some forests are not economically accessible so only 25 million m^3 are harvested for domestic use. Japan will probably continue its wood imports amounting to approximately 59 million m^3 ha per year.
- An estimate of the Chinese forest area is approximately 130 million ha. Fuel wood is the biggest potential source of industrial wood.
- Asia and the Pacific Rim countries will continue to be the world's largest wood deficit area in the foreseeable future. Production of tropical logs will decrease, and production of industrial wood particularly hardwood for pulp from Indonesia will increase.

CHAPTER 3

Sources

1 Food and Agriculture Organisation of the United Nations (FAO)
2 Jaakko Pöyry Consulting Oy
3 Finnish Forest Industry Federation
4 Swedish Forest Industries Association

CHAPTER 4

Raw material resources – secondary fiber supply

1	Introduction	48
2	Definitions	48
3	Global recovery, demand and supply	51
4	Western Europe	55
4.1	Recovery and utilization	55
4.2	Recovered paper prices	57
4.3	Collection organizations	58
	Sources	59

CHAPTER 4

Raw material resources – secondary fiber supply

1 Introduction

Recycled fiber is an important raw material for the forest industry whose use is growing rapidly. In 1970, the share of recycled fiber in the global fiber furnish composition excluding mineral additives was 20%. In 1995, it had increased to 35%. It is expected to grow to approximately 40% by 2010[1].

In the 1960s and 1970s, recycled fiber was mainly used as a local substitute for virgin fiber on old, small paper machines. Recycled fiber today is a preferred raw material used on modern machines for grades where its use was previously unthinkable. The following factors have been the driving force behind this development:

1. A growing need and determination to reduce the volume of solid waste for landfill.
2. Legislation covering the separate collection of used packaging materials of paper and board resulted in large quantities of recovered paper of rather low grade and quality.
3. New technology in the areas of deinking, screening of impurities, fractionation, bleaching, and paper web forming helped the industry increase the consumption of recovered paper.
4. Consumer awareness on environmental issues and acceptance of recycled products has increased.
5. Large scale recycling projects have become economically attractive.

2 Definitions

Recycled fiber has two main categories:
1. **Pre-consumer waste** refers to paper or board residues collected from converters, printers, distributors, and transportation organizations before using the paper or board for its intended end use.
2. **Post-consumer waste** includes paper or board consumed by various end users collected from households, offices, retail trade, etc.

Raw material resources – secondary fiber supply

Recovery rate and **utilization rate** are two concepts used in making comparisons of the relative importance of recycled fiber in different countries. The following equations provide the concepts for these definitions:

$$\text{Recovery rate of a given region } (\%) = 100 \times \frac{\text{recycled fibre collection}}{\text{paper and board consumption}} \quad (1)$$

$$\text{Utilization rate of a given region } (\%) = 100 \times \frac{\text{recycled fibre consuption}}{\text{paper and board production}} \quad (2)$$

Calculation of the utilization rate does not include the normal fiber losses of 10–25%.

Table 1 gives a detailed Confederation of European Paper Industries (CEPI) classification of recovered paper grades.

Table 1. List of European standard qualities of recovered paper.

LIST OF EUROPEAN STANDARD QUALITIES OF RECOVERED PAPER	
Group A - Ordinary qualities	**Group B - Medium qualities**
A 0 - Unsorted mixed waste paper Including unsorted consolidated material from households, no guarantee of absence of unusable materials	**B 1 - Once-read news** Old newspapers, with less than 5 % color inserts or advertisements. Total of unusable materials: max. 1 %
A 1 - Mixed papers and boards (unsorted) A mixture of various grades of paper and board, without restriction on short fiber content. Total of unusable materials: max. 1 %	**B 2 - Overissue news** Unsold daily newspapers, printed on white newsprint and free from additional color inserts or illustrated material, strings allowed.
A 2 - Mixed papers and boards (sorted) A mixture of various qualities of paper and board, containing less that 40 % of newspapers and magazines. Total of unusable materials: max. 1 %	**B 3 - White lined board cuttings** New cuttings of multi-ply board with at least one white liner over a grey interior or back.
A 3 - Board cuttings Shavings and cuttings of chipboard or mixed boards, free from strawboard and corrugated material.	**B 4 - Mixed colored shavings** Printers or magazine shavings, without restrictions as to color, mechanical pulp or coated paper content.

CHAPTER 4

Table 1. List of European standard qualities of recovered paper.

LIST OF EUROPEAN STANDARD QUALITIES OF RECOVERED PAPER	
A 4 - Supermarket waste User paper and board packaging containing at least 70 % of corrugated board, the rest being solid boards and wrapping papers. Total of unusable materials: max. 1 %	**B 5 - Bookbinders shavings** White shavings, printed with various colors, mainly mechanical pulp based paper, with or without adhesive bindings.
A 5 - Corrugated container waste Used cases, sheets or cuttings of corrugated board. Total of unusable materials: max. 1 %	**B 6 - Bookbinders shavings without adhesive** White shavings, printed with various colors, mainly mechanical pulp based paper, free from adhesive bindings
A 6 - New shavings of corrugated board New shavings of corrugated board free from any other paper and any trace of unusable material; they are crushed or shredded and are guaranteed to be free from contact with any other product.	**B 7 - Colored letters** Correspondence, in mixed colors, with or without print, of printing or writing paper. Free from carbon paper and hard covers. Total of unusable materials: max. 1 %
A 7 - Overissue pamphlets and magazines Unsold pamphlets and magazines, with or without adhesive binding, strings allowed.	**B 8 - White woodfree books** Books, without hard covers, of woodfree white paper, black printed only. Not to contain more than 10 % coated paper. Total of unusable materials: max. 1 %
A 8 - Overissue pamphlets and magazines free from adhesive bindings A mixture of unsold newspapers and pamphlets, free from adhesive bindings, strings allowed.	**B 9 - Bookquire** Woodfree misprints of books, black and white printed.
A 9 - Mixed news and pamphlets A mixture of newspaper and pamphlets with at least 50 % of news, with or without adhesive bindings, strings allowed.	**B 10 - Colored best pams** White or colored, coated or uncoated periodicals and brochures, free from non-flexible covers, bindings, varnishes, non-dispersable inks and adhesives, poster papers, labels or label trim. May include heavily printed circulars and colored shavings. Mechanical content less than 10 %.
A 10 - News and pamphlets free from adhesive bindings A mixture of newspaper and pamphlets, with at least 60 % of news, free from adhesive bindings, strings allowed.	**B 11 - White carbonless copy papers** White carbonless copy papers
A 11 - Mixed pams and magazines Mixed once read pamphlets, magazines, catalogues, printed matter, directories and newspapers, with or without staples, free from hard cover. Total of unusable materials: max. 1 %	**B 12 - Colored carbonless copy papers** colored carbonless copy papers.
	B 13 - Coated board Polyethylene coated board from liquid packaging board manufacturers.

CEPAC 1990

Raw material resources – secondary fiber supply

To make global comparisons possible and meaningful, the Food and Agriculture Organization of the United Nations (FAO) and Organization for Economic Cooperation and Development (OECD) systems are often applied as follows:

1. Old and over-issued newspapers and magazines, telephone directories, etc., containing mainly mechanical pulp.
2. Corrugated and solid container waste, kraft bags, etc., containing mainly unbleached sulfate pulp.
3. Woodfree printing and writing papers, punch cards, bleached board cuttings from converters, etc.
4. All other types such as mixed papers and boards.

3 Global recovery, demand and supply

Figure 1 shows the global recovery and consumption of recycled paper in 1993[2].

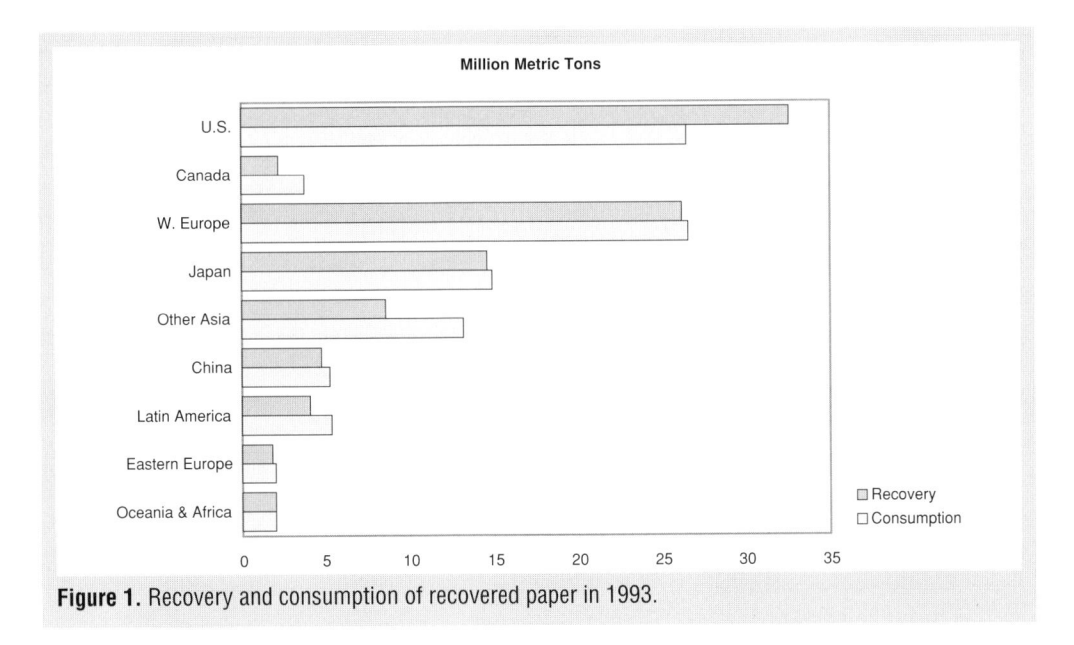

Figure 1. Recovery and consumption of recovered paper in 1993.

1. In 1993, the United States led with paper recovery at 33 million tons. Consumption was 26 million tons and exports approximately 7 million tons. Of the exported material, 3.6 million tons went to Asia and the Pacific Rim countries, 2.7 million tons went to Canada, and the remainder to Europe. The 3.6 million tons constituted approximately 70% of the recycled fiber imports to Asia and the Pacific Rim countries with the rest coming predominantly from Europe.
2. With the exception of Canada and Asia and the Pacific Rim countries, most regions were approximately equal in recovery and consumption in 1993.
3. Although balanced in aggregate terms, Europe has a total flow of recovered paper within Europe of 4 million tons per year[1].

CHAPTER 4

Table 2 shows the global recovery and utilization rates developed during 1971–1991[1].

Table 2. Recovery and utilization rates of recycled fiber by main world regions 1971–1991.

Region	Recovery rate 1971 %	Recovery rate 1981 %	Recovery rate 1991 %	Utilization rate 1971 %	Utilization rate 1981 %	Utilization rate 1991 %
North America	22.6	26.2	35.9	20.6	21.8	26.9
Western Europe	28.3	33.8	39.3	27.6	32.0	38.3
Nordic	22.4	32.4	42.2	5.4	7.6	8.8
Western Europe excl. Nordic countries	28.6	33.9	39.1	36.7	43.3	50.9
Eastern Europe & CIS	20.0	26.1	29.0	20.1	25.0	28.0
Oceania	21.1	25.9	32.0	25.6	31.1	34.0
Latin America	23.9	27.6	33.0	37.1	41.9	46.0
Japan	37.4	47.2	50.4	36.7	47.1	53.4
China	12.8	13.1	26.0	12.9	14.2	32.0
Rest of Asia	14.2	30.5	37.0	29.0	60.4	70.0
Africa	19.2	18.8	23.0	36.6	31.5	33.0
Total	**24.7**	**29.8**	**37.0**	**24.7**	**29.6**	**37.5**

Table 2 shows two main facts:
1. The global recovery rate has increased from 25% in 1971 to 37% in 1991. Japan had the highest recovery rate at 50%, and Africa had the lowest at 23%.
2. The global utilization rate increased proportionately with the recovery rate from 25% to 38% during the 20–year period beginning in 1971. China had the highest rate at 70% and the Nordic countries the lowest at 9%.

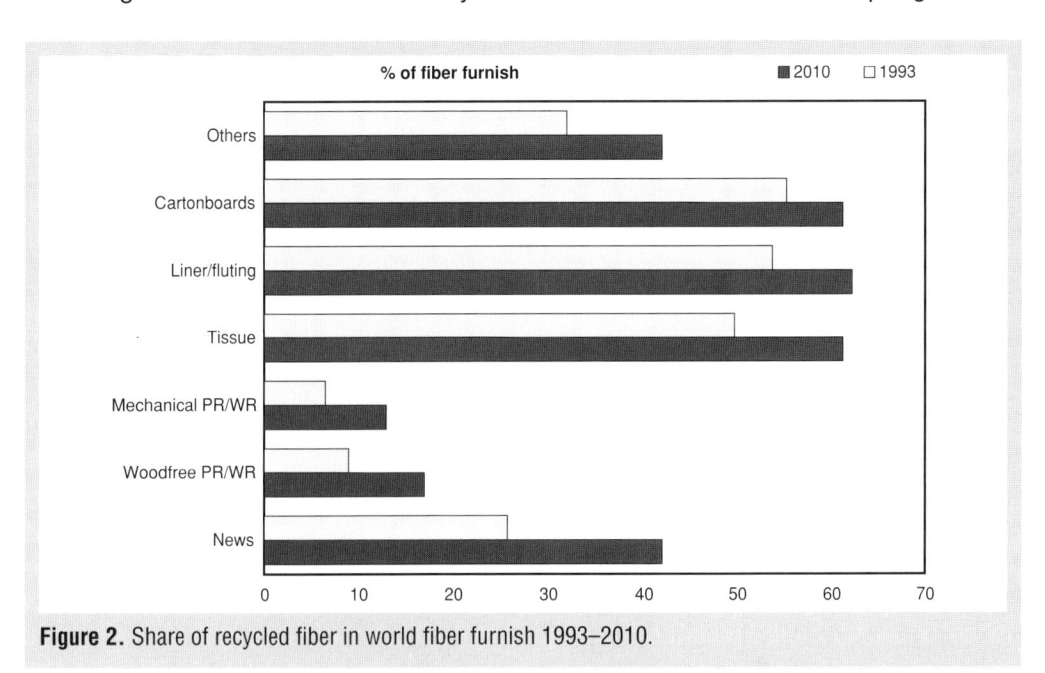

Raw material resources – secondary fiber supply

Figure 2 shows the share of recycled fiber in the world fiber furnish per grade[1]:

Figure 2. Share of recycled fiber in world fiber furnish 1993–2010.

1. In 1993, the share of recycled fiber was highest in tissue at approximately 48%, in linerboard and fluting at approximately 53%, and in cartonboards at approximately 53%. The share of recycled fiber in all these grades will probably exceed 60% by 2010.
2. In newsprint, the share of recycled fiber was 25% in 1993. This figure is expected to increase to over 40% by 2010.
3. For printing and writing papers both woodfree and mechanical, the share of recycled fiber in the furnish is and will remain modest at 10–20%.

In the future, the global recovery rates should grow rapidly, from 37% in 1991 to 48% in 2010 as Figure 3 suggests[1].

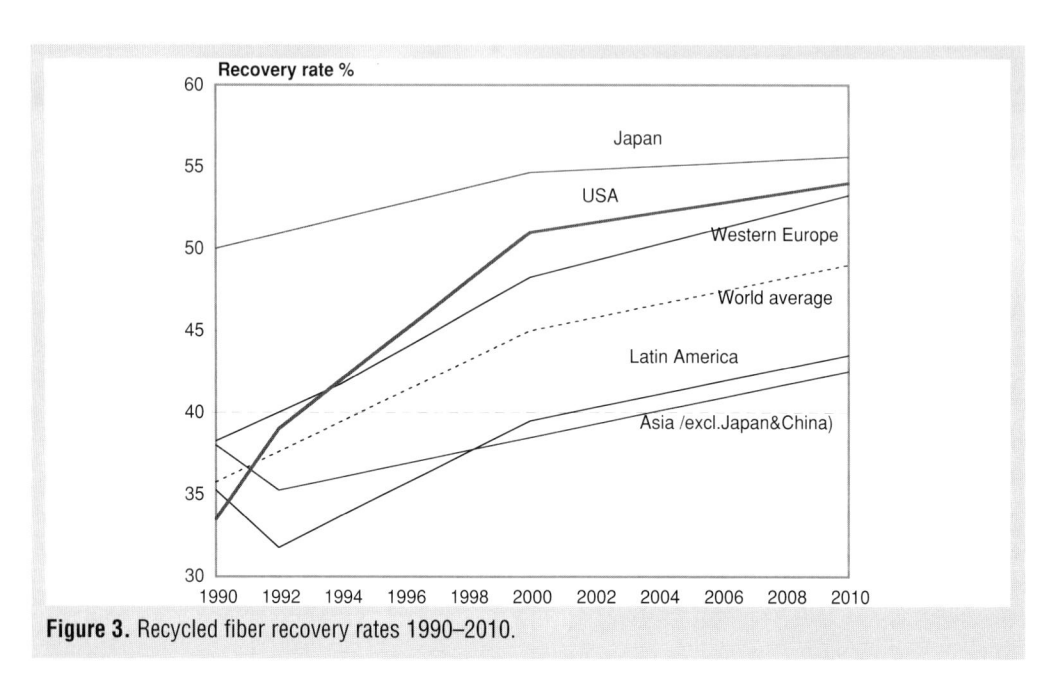

CHAPTER 4

Figure 3. Recycled fiber recovery rates 1990–2010.

The increase in the recovery rate will be particularly significant in the United States where the 50% mark should be reached before 2000. In Japan, the present recovery rate of approximately 50% will probably flatten and increase only moderately to 55% by 2010.

If these projections materialize, net trading in recycled fiber in 1992–2010 will change as Figure 4 indicates[1].

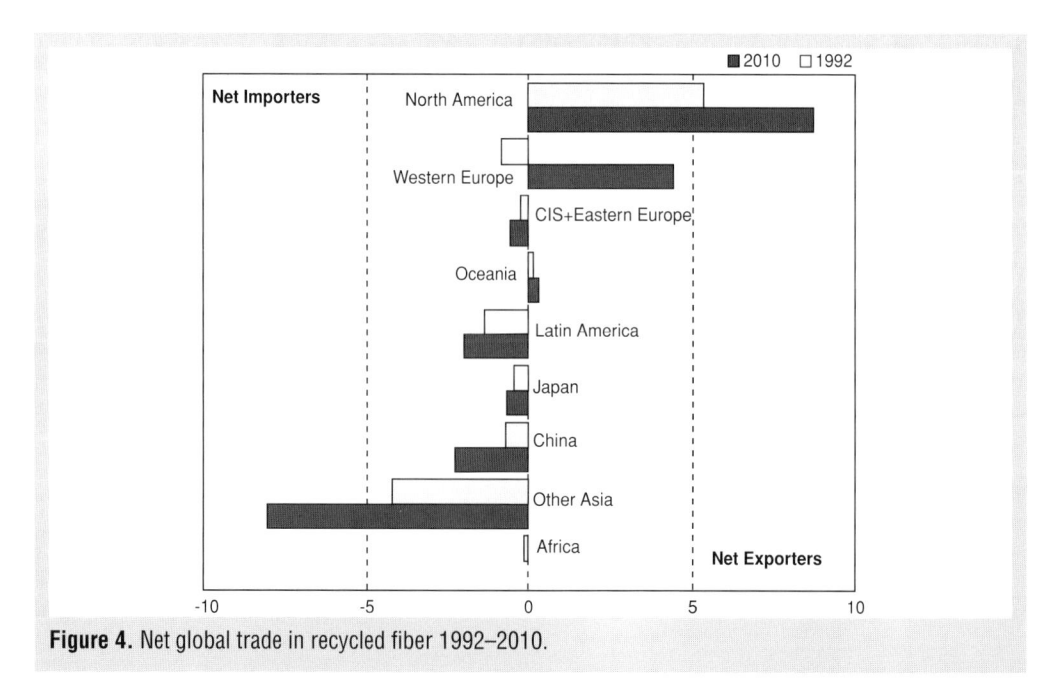

Figure 4. Net global trade in recycled fiber 1992–2010.

In 2010 there will be two major exporting areas – North America with approximately 8 million tons and Europe with approximately 4 million tons – and one large importing area – Asia and the Pacific Rim countries with imports of approximately 11 million tons from the above regions. These trade flows are significant and necessary to satisfy the anticipated growing regional fiber requirements.

The examples in Table 3 show the importance of recycled fibers in the global fiber supply.

Table 3. Example of impact of recovery rate of recycled fiber on global fiber supply.

Impact of recovery rate of recycled fiber on global fiber supply	1993 million tons	2010
1. Paper and board consumption	240	400
2. Recycled fiber recovery	91	152
3. Recovery rate (%)	38	38
4. Alternative recovery rates in 2010		
4.1. 40 %		160
4.2. 48 %		192
4.3. 55 %		220

Assuming a recovery rate increase from 38% to 48% between 1993 and 2010, the table shows that recycled fiber will replace 40 million tons of virgin fiber. A deviation of only one percentage point in the recovery rate will change the demand for virgin fiber by ± 4 million tons per year.

4 Western Europe

4.1 Recovery and utilization

As Table 2 shows, Western Europe led recycled paper recovery second only to Japan. Figure 5 shows the recovery and use trends since 1971.

The figure shows that
1. In 1970 the recovery rate was 28%. It increased to 38% by the early 1990s and to 42% by the mid 1990s – approximately 0.5 percentage points per year.
2. This trend should continue for at least another 10 years.
3. The development in the utilization rate has been parallel to that of the recovery rate.

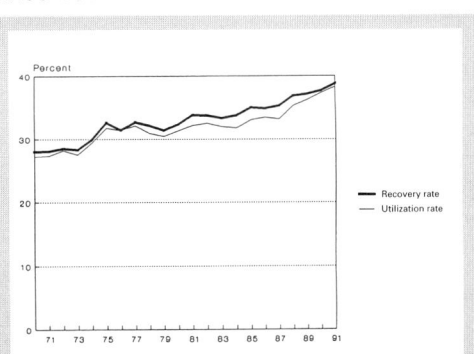

Figure 5. Recycled fiber recovery and use trends in 1970–1991 for western Europe.

CHAPTER 4

Figure 6 illustrates the use of recycled fiber in various grades in the early 1990s.

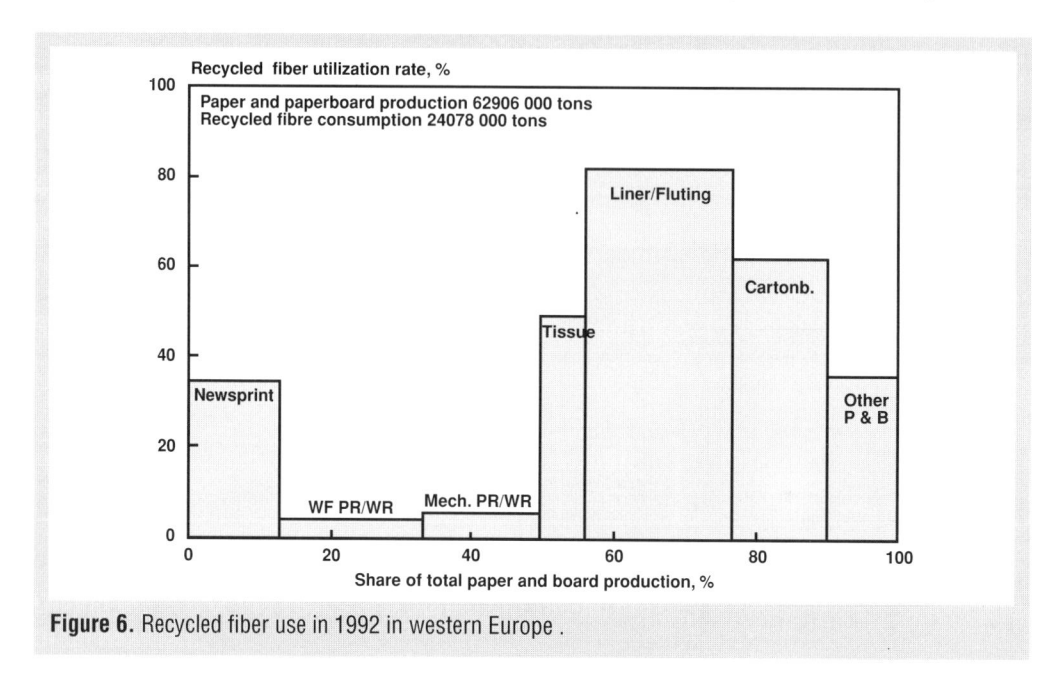

Figure 6. Recycled fiber use in 1992 in western Europe.

The following conclusions can be made:
1. Linerboard and fluting had the highest utilization rate of approximately 80%, followed by cartonboards at 60% and tissue at 50%. Considering that these figures include the Nordic countries with only small domestic recovered fiber sources, the rate in Central Europe must be nearly 100%. This is substantiated by the fact that Germany – the largest producer in Europe – has reached the 100% level for many grades. Figure 7 shows the rate of recycled fiber use in Germany.

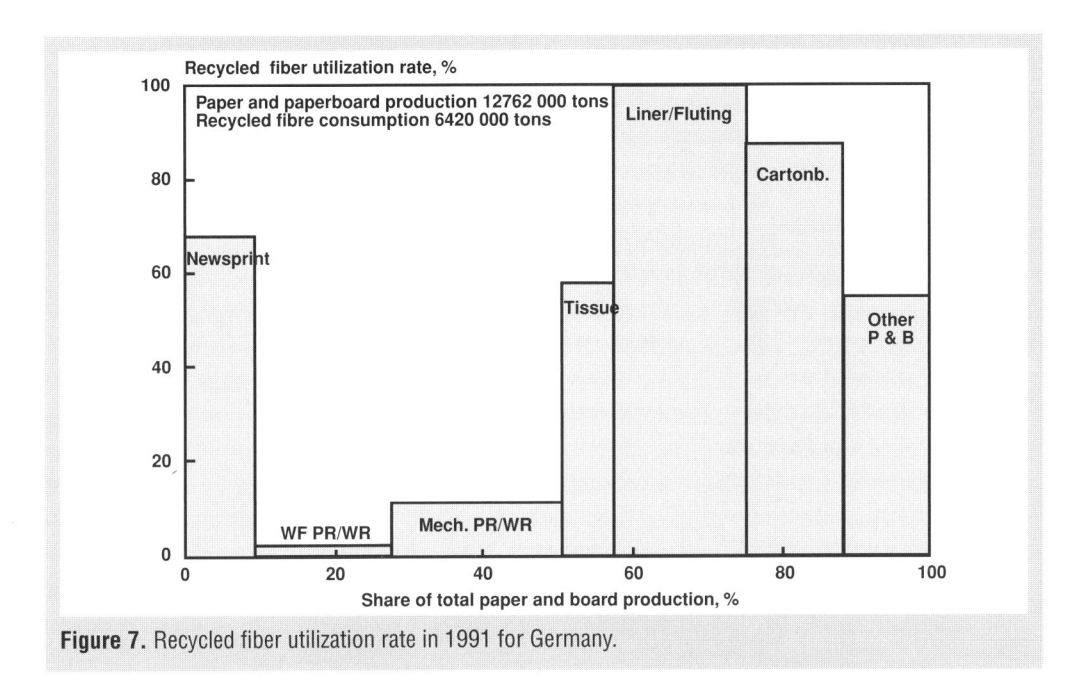

Figure 7. Recycled fiber utilization rate in 1991 for Germany.

2. This means that any future capacity expansion in Europe will largely depend on increased consumption of paper and an increased recovery of recycled fiber.

One estimate is that the total fiber recovery in western Europe will increase from 24 million tons in 1991 to 35 million tons in 2000, with a respective increase in the recovery rate from 39% to 47%.

4.2 Recovered paper prices

Recovered paper prices have two main characteristics:
1. The prices fluctuate considerably. Fluctuations within 1:3 or even 1:4 are possible during periods shorter than twelve months.
2. The trends for prices have declined both in nominal and in real terms.

In the future, the growing exports of recycled fiber to Asia and the Pacific Rim countries are new factors that will probably influence price developments in Europe. One scenario is that the Asian buyers will play North American and European suppliers against each other by alternating purchases. This will depress prices during periods of no or low purchases and have the opposite effect during high purchases. The outcome would be more rather than less price fluctuations in the future. Another scenario is that the increased demand of recovered paper in Asia and the Pacific Rim countries will permanently increase purchases from Europe resulting in a rising price trend.

4.3 Collection organizations

Mills usually collect and handle pre-consumer waste as return loads for large converters or by merchants on a regular contract basis.

Germany, Netherlands, and Sweden officially organized post-consumer collection of recovered paper from households in the early 1990s. It includes separation of white and brown waste. In other countries, recovered paper collection is mostly in the hands of voluntary organizations, although the trend in most European countries is toward industrial trade organizations.

In Germany, the biggest recovered paper collector is the paper industry. It is responsible for handling the collection and recycling of packaging according to the Duales System Deutschland (DSD). It is also typical that several energy companies such as RWE/Trineken have acquired waste disposal companies since paper is likely to play a role as a source of energy.

Table 4 lists the 13 largest recovered paper merchants in Europe in 1994[2].

Table 4. Largest recovered paper merchants in Europe 1994.

Company	Merchant	Estimated trade volume 1000 tons	Location
KNP BT	Lignac & Lewison, Birmingham waste	1500	D, NL, UK, A
SCA	De Hoop. SCA Recycling UK, Italmaceri, Bunzl & Blach, Papyrus, PWA Itpapier	1400	NL, UK, I, S, D
SKP	SKP, SKP van Gelder	1400	D, NL
Generales des Eaux	Soulier (ONYX)	1300	F
Mayr-Meinhof	Meltra	1000	D, A
Jefferson Smurfit	CDI, Smurfit Waste Paper. Ireland Recl.	960	F, UK, IR
BPB	Davidsons Waste Paper, J. de Paauw	900	UK, NL
Trinekens	Ho-Pa-Ge, Fisher	900	D
David S. Smith	Severnside Waste / St. Regis	1100	UK
Haindl	Ropa, Parenco Oud Papier	750	D, NL
Stone Container	Julius Rhode, Cheshire Recycling	700	D, UK
E. Bohm		500	D
Weig	Nord-Westdeutsche Papierrohstuff	375	D

Five merchant groups have a trade volume over one million tons. Paper companies own seven of the largest 13 and have integrated their operations. Integration between recovered paper merchants and the paper industry is likely to continue, although energy companies, local communities and cities also aim for a share in the recovered paper market.

Sources

1. Jaakko Pöyry Consulting Oy
2. Various industrial sources

CHAPTER 5

World paper markets

1	**Introduction**	**61**
2	**Definitions**	**61**
2.1	Bulk and special products	61
2.2	Specification of main paper grades	63
3	**Driving forces of demand**	**65**
4	**Global paper demand**	**66**
5	**International trade flows in 1993**	**68**
6	**Price trends 1980–1995**	**69**
6.1	General	69
6.2	Newsprint and mechanical printing paper	69
6.3	Woodfree printing and writing papers	70
6.4	Corrugated raw materials	70
6.5	Cartonboards	71
6.6	Price stability in Germany 1980–1993	71
7	**Selection criteria for manufacturing**	**72**
	Sources	75

World paper markets

1 Introduction

Paper is an integral part of daily life in most parts of the world. Global paper consumption has grown from 43 million tons in 1950 to 260 million tons in 1995. This is a rate of 4.1%, or 4.8 million tons per year. Growth has exceeded Gross Domestic Production (GDP) growth since 1950 by a factor of 1–1.5 depending on time, period and region. The most rapidly growing areas have been China, Japan, Asia and Latin America where the growth rate has clearly been above average.

2 Definitions

2.1 Bulk and special products

The typical features of bulk products are
- large market volumes
- similar quality requirements which make it possible for the end user to interchange the products of different suppliers

The sales price is the single most important competitive factor for a bulk paper producer. The producers that have the lowest manufacturing costs globally and a sufficiently large market share determine the sales price of bulk paper products during normal balance of demand and supply or in an oversupply situation. The price in such situations establishes itself at an equal global level, considering the transport costs to different regions. Particularly in oversupply situations, the price level decreases to the cash cost level of the lowest cost producers.

During healthy upswings in demand that cause a positive balance of supply and demand – usually temporary in the forest industry – supply and demand determine the price. It has little or no correlation with manufacturing costs. A typical example of this phenomenon was the price increase of pulp in 1994 and 1995, when the price for softwood kraft pulp increased from USD 400/ton to USD 1000/ton within less than 24 months. Then it fell below USD 500/ton in less than 6 months during early 1996.

One can therefore conclude that bulk grade production is raw material and production oriented. Development efforts often concentrate on increasing efficiency in the manufacturing process.

CHAPTER 5

The typical features of specialty products are
- market volumes are small
- quality requirements differ from one end user to another
- quality levels of different producers differ
- price levels vary with application and user.

Significant factors affecting competition besides price level are the following:
- quality level
- delivery time
- technical service
- reliability of above factors.

Specialty products are higher value-added products with higher prices. Their production is market oriented, and research concentrates on improving quality level and service.

Many specialities have grown with time into bulk products. This increases the importance of price as a competitive factor. A typical example of a paper grade that has experienced this development is coated woodfree paper. This has to a large extent started to change from speciality to bulk product in the mid 1980s. The process is slow and gradual. In the 1990s, there are still segments of coated woodfree papers that are clearly speciality items, but most consumption is bulk product.

The line differentiating bulk grades from specialities is not clear. Table 1 is an attempt to provide examples of certain bulk grades and speciality items.

Table 1. Examples of bulk and speciality items.

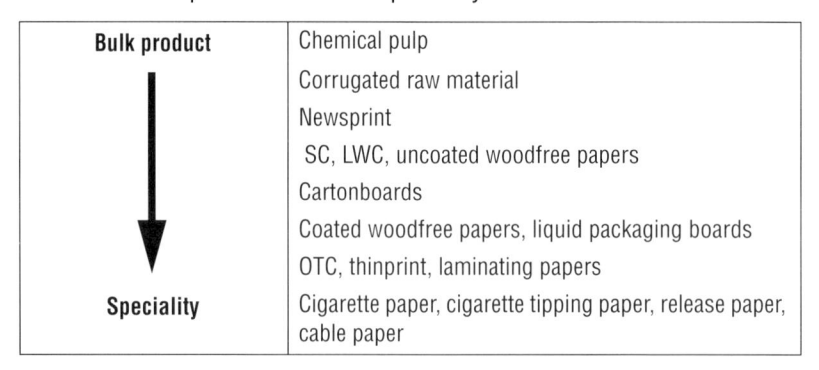

Bulk product ↓ **Speciality**	Chemical pulp
	Corrugated raw material
	Newsprint
	SC, LWC, uncoated woodfree papers
	Cartonboards
	Coated woodfree papers, liquid packaging boards
	OTC, thinprint, laminating papers
	Cigarette paper, cigarette tipping paper, release paper, cable paper

2.2 Specification of main paper grades

Table 2 summarizes the most important paper grades as well as their furnish composition and substance range.

Table 2. Furnish composition and substance range of main paper grades.

Quality	Basis weight g/m²	SW	Chemical pulp HW	Mechanical pulp	Waste paper	Minerals and additives
		\multicolumn{5}{c}{% of total fiber}				
Newsprint (waste based)	40–45–52			0–50	50–100	<10
Newsprint (virgin fiber)	40–45–52	0–10		90–100		<5
Uncoated mechanical papers	50–56–60	10–25		75–90		15–30
Coated mechanical papers	40–56–80	30–40		60–70		30–35
Uncoated woodfree papers	50–80–140	20–50	50–80			20–30
Coated woodfree papers	90–100–150	30–60	40–70			20–30
Tissue	20–60					
Liner						
- kraftliner	115–250					
- testliner	90–150					100	
Fluting						
- SC fluting	90–150					
- wellenstoff	90–150					100	
Sackpaper	50–100					
Cartonboards						
- folding boxboard	150–400			50–75		10–20
- white lined chipboard	150–400				50–75	10–20
Others						

The main characteristics of the grades are the following:
1. Newsprint:
   Newsprint is mainly used for newspaper manufacture – approximately 80% – and almost exclusively in reels. The global demand in 1993 was 33 million tons. Its main quality characteristics are stable quality and good runnability. Recovered paper use in furnish has increased dramatically during the last decade.
2. Uncoated mechanical papers – mainly supercalandered (SC):
   SC paper is used for magazines and advertising materials mainly in reels. Stable quality, a smooth printing surface for four color printing, and good runability are the most important quality characteristics. Global demand in 1993 was 12 million tons. Printing methods are offset and rotogravure.

3. Coated mechanical papers – mainly light weight coated (LWC):
   Coated mechanical papers find the same uses as SC papers and also mainly in reels. High brightness is an additional quality factor for these papers. Global demand in 1993 was 12 million tons. The printing methods are the same as for SC papers.
4. Uncoated woodfree papers:
   These grades are used for printing and copying paper (A4), offset printing for books and brochures, continuous forms, etc. High brightness, stable quality and good formation are the most important quality requirements. Global demand in 1993 was 37 million tons. End users in this market usually make their purchases from wholesale merchants.
5. Coated woodfree papers:
   These grades are for high quality four color printing such as books, brochures, advertising materials and magazines. Two-thirds of the consumption is sheets and the remainder is in reels. Global demand in 1993 was 14 million tons. Wholesale merchants sell a major part of this to end users.
6. Tissue:
   Tissue is used for hygienic purposes such as toilet paper, napkins, kitchen towels, facial tissues, handkerchiefs, etc. Global demand in 1993 was 15 million tons. The proportion of recycled fiber in the furnish of these grades is high and increasing (approximately 50% globally in the middle 1990s).
7. Corrugating materials:
   Kraft and testliner have the same use – the outer and inner layers of corrugated board. Kraftliner is virgin fiberboard and test liner is recovered board. Stable quality and good strength properties are the main quality characteristics. Semichemical fluting (SC fluting) and wellenstoff are used for the middle layer of corrugated board. SC fluting is virgin board, and wellenstoff is based on recovered materials.
   Global demand for corrugating materials in 1993 was 70 million tons.
8. Sack paper:
   Sack paper is used for sacks and bags. Good strength properties and suitable porosity are the main quality characteristics. Global demand in 1993 was 5 million tons.
9. Cartonboards:
   Cartonboards are for packaging boxes for food, beverages, cosmetics, chemicals, etc., usually consisting of two or more layers. The outer layer is usually of chemical pulp and the middle layers either of mechanical pulp or recovered paper. When mechanical pulp is used, the product is folding boxboard (FBB). If the middle layer contains recycled fiber, the product is white lined chipboard (WLC). Both coated and uncoated cartonboards are produced. Global demand in 1993 was 25 million tons.

3 Driving forces of demand

In the 1960s and 1970s, the main driving forces of paper demand were economic factors, demographic data, and industrial production. During the following two decades, additional factors became increasingly important. These included application developments, substitution factors, basis weight development, office technology, and advertising expenditure. Any reliable forecast must consider all these factors when predicting the future.

The most important factor has been and remains economic development usually measured by GDP. The reliability of any analysis of future developments therefore depends on the accuracy of estimating this factor. Figure 1 illustrates the strong correlation of GDP per capita and paper consumption.

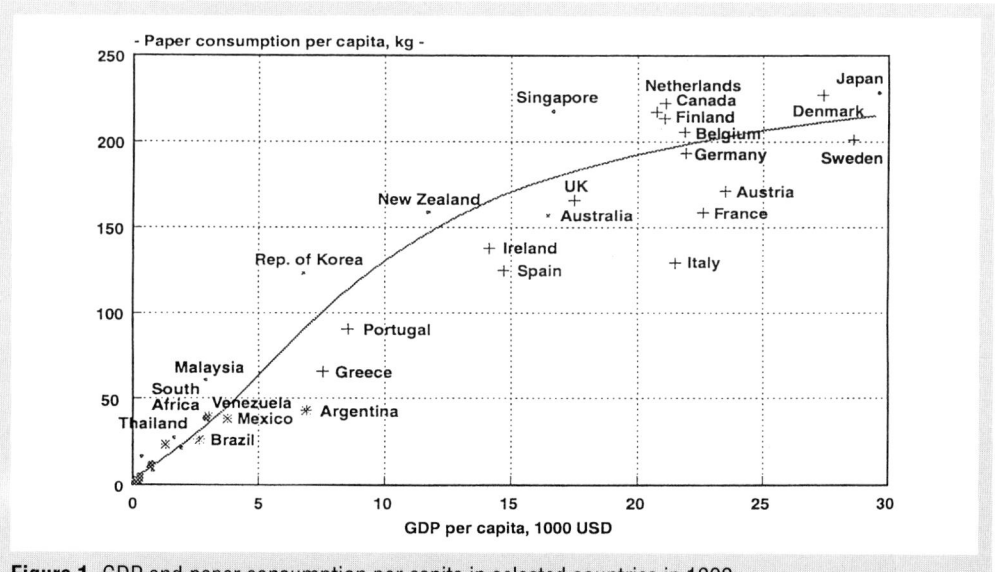

Figure 1. GDP and paper consumption per capita in selected countries in 1992.

CHAPTER 5

4 Global paper demand

Figures 2 and 3 show the forecast growth rate of global paper demand for the period 1993–2010 by grade and region.

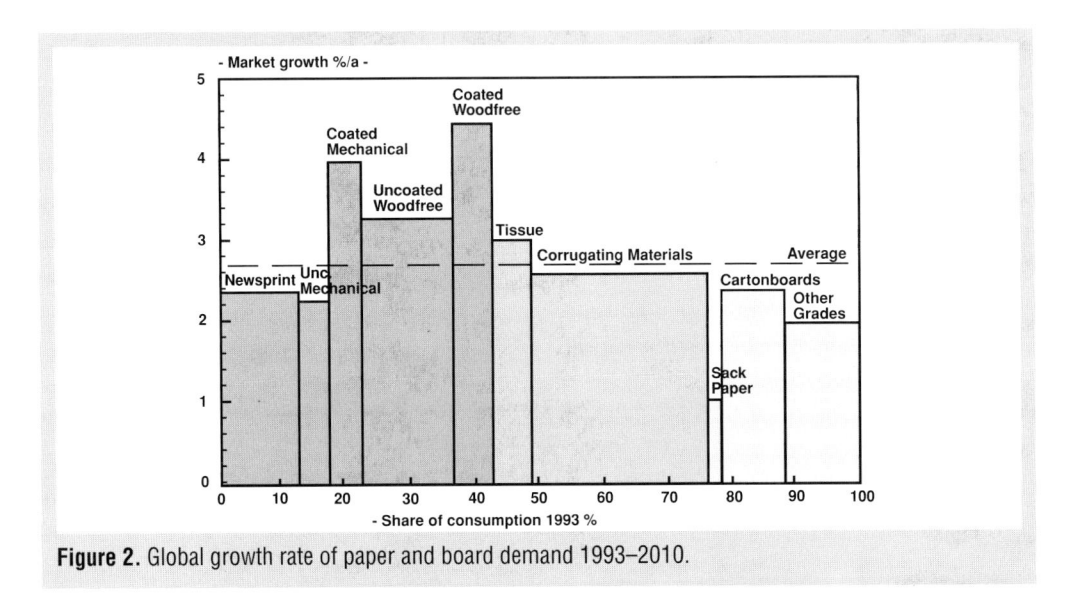

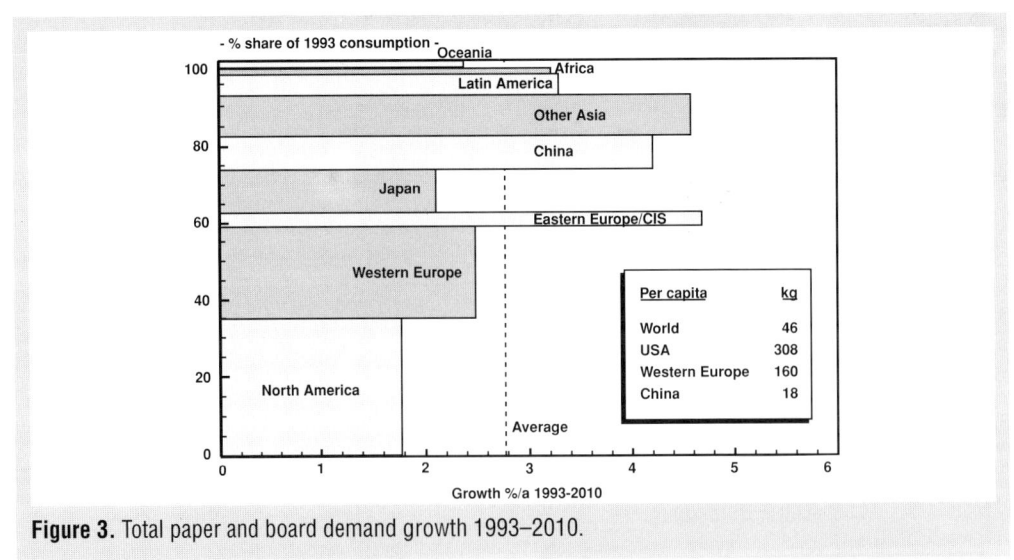

Figure 2. Global growth rate of paper and board demand 1993–2010.

Figure 3. Total paper and board demand growth 1993–2010.

The following trends are apparent in the forecasts:
1. The fastest growth by grade should occur in coated woodfree papers at 4.4% per year and in coated mechanical papers at 3.9% per year. Low growth rates will occur in sack paper and other grades amounting to 1–2% per year.

World paper markets

2. Regional growth will be rapid in Asia, China and Eastern Europe at 4–5% per year. North America and Japan will experience a relatively slow growth rate of less than 2% per year.

According to the above growth rates by grade and region, global paper demand will develop as Figure 4 shows.

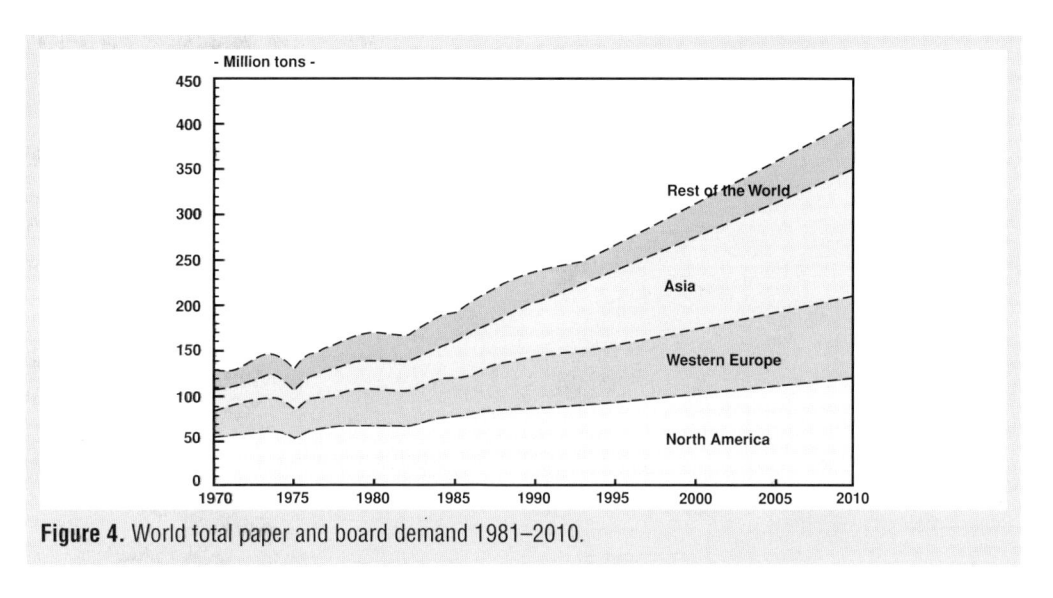

Figure 4. World total paper and board demand 1981–2010.

Global paper demand will therefore increase from 253 million tons in 1993 to 402 million tons in 2010. This is a rate of 2.8% or 8.8 million tons per year.

Table 3 shows the expected demand for main grades.

Table 3. Growth of demand for main paper grades 1993–2010.

	1993 million tns	2010 million tns	Growth rate % / a
Newsprint	32.6	48.3	2.3
Uncoated mechanical papers	12.3	18.0	2.2
Coated mechanical papers	11.9	22.9	3.9
Uncoated woodfree papers	37.2	64.1	3.3
Coated woodfree papers	14.4	30.1	4.4
Tissue	15.1	25.0	3.0
Corrugated materials	70.0	108.4	2.6
Sackpaper	5.1	6.1	1.1
Cartonboards	25.4	38.8	2.5
Others	28.8	40.3	2.0
Total	**252.8**	**402.0**	**2.8**

CHAPTER 5

5 International trade flows in 1993

Table 4 summarizes the trade flows for the main paper grades.

Table 4. Main exporting and importing countries per grade 1993.

	Main exporters	mill. tons	**Main importers**	mill. tons
Newsprint	Canada	8.0	USA	5.9
	Sweden	1.9	UK	1.4
	Finland	1.2	Germany	1.2
	USA	0.9	Japan	0.5
	Norway	0.8	France	0.4
Top 5 exporters' share of global demand 39 %				
Uncoated mechanical papers	Canada	1.9	USA	2.4
	Finland	1.6	Germany	1
	Austria	0.4	UK	0.5
	Germany	0.4	France	0.4
	Norway	0.4	Italy	0.3
	Sweden	0.3	Netherlands	0.2
Top 5 exporters' share of global demand 41 %				
Coated mechanical papers	Finland	1.8	USA	0.8
	Germany	0.7	Germany	0.7
	Italy	0.4	UK	0.6
	France	0.4	France	0.5
	Belgium	0.4	Spain	0.3
Top 5 exporters' share of global demand 31 %				
Uncoated woodfree papers	Finland	1.1	USA	1.0
	Canada	0.8	Germany	0.8
	USA	0.6	UK	0.5
	Brazil	0.6	France	0.4
	Germany	0.6	Italy	0.4
Top 5 exporters' share of global demand 10 %				
Coated woodfree papers	Finland	0.6	UK	0.5
	Germany	0.6	Germany	0.4
	Austria	0.5	France	0.4
	France	0.4	Belgium	0.3
	Sweden	0.3	USA	0.3
Top 5 exporters' share of global demand 17 %				
Kraftliner	USA	2.7	Germany	0.7
	Sweden	1.3	UK	0.7
	Canada	0.5	Italy	0.5
	Brazil	0.4	Hong Kong	0.4

Trade flows are small especially for woodfree papers. Woodfree papers are therefore primarily domestic in nature.

6 Price trends 1980–1995

6.1 General

The nominal price trends of most paper grades develop positively due to weakening currency values. To remove the effect of inflation from a nominal price series, one uses a deflating factor. This is usually a wholesale or producers' price index. The following analysis made for the German forest industry uses real 1995 monetary values.

6.2 Newsprint and mechanical printing paper

Figure 5. Newsprint and mechanical printing paper prices in Germany 1980–1995.

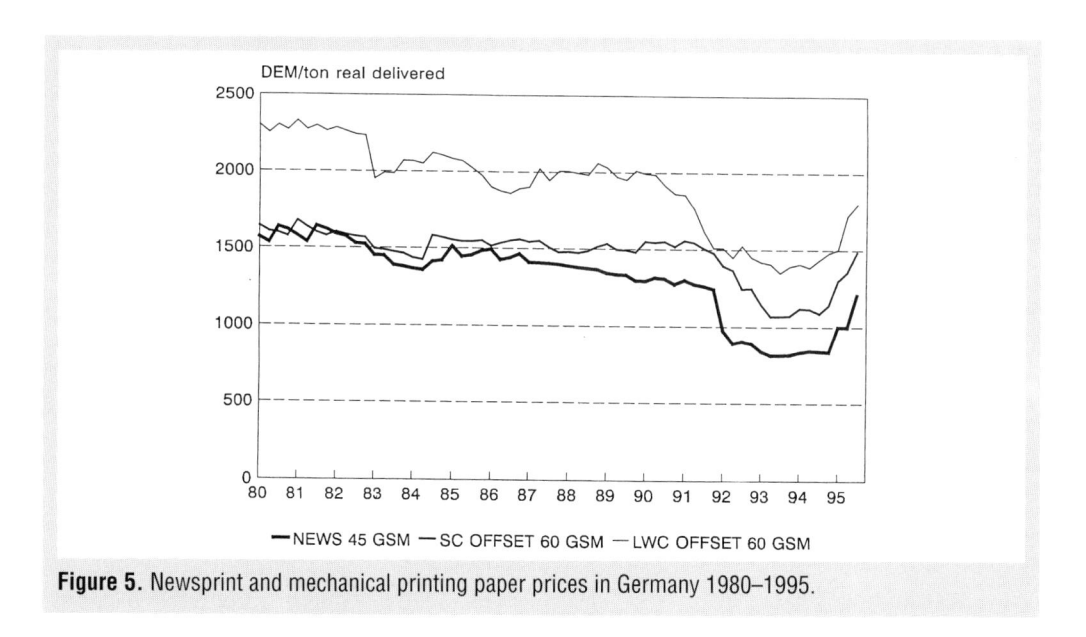

Figure 5 shows that for 1980–1991 newsprint prices were relatively stable with a slight declining trend from DEM 1600/ton to DEM 1300/ton. This stability was due to annual or semi annual contracts between large newspaper publishers and newsprint manufacturers and traditionally good price discipline.

In 1992, newsprint prices collapsed to DEM 800/ton for two years. In 1995 prices increased again above the DEM 1000/ton level without reaching the price level of 1991. One reason for this development was cheap local recycled fiber raw material and local modern paper machines with low manufacturing costs.

The trend for SC and LWC papers has been very similar to that of newsprint. This is mostly due to the fact that the demand fluctuation is similar to the above grades and that these grades are to some extent interchangeable especially in the case of SC and LWC papers.

CHAPTER 5

6.3 Woodfree printing and writing papers

Woodfree paper prices have followed the price trends of chemical pulp but with slightly less fluctuation. Uncoated grades such as A4 cut size achieved peak prices in 1981–1982 at DEM 2400/ton. Rockbottom was reached in 1993, when prices for uncoated grades were approximately DEM 1200–1300/ton – half the 1981–1982 peak level. According to the information in Figure 6, the price trend for woodfree papers is declining slightly now.

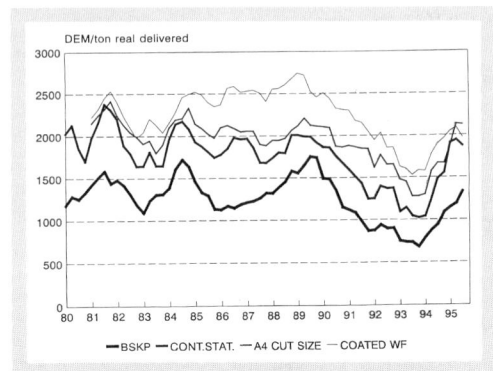

Figure 6. Real prices of woodfree paper in Germany 1980–1995.

Coated woodfree papers reached peak prices in 1988–1989. The price was then DEM 2700/ton. The bottom level was in 1992 at DEM 1500/ton. Some recovery has taken place since then, but it is likely that price trends for coated woodfree papers will decrease due to the large, efficient paper machines that have entered the market in 1993–1997. These include Enso PM6 and PM7 in Oulu, Burgo/Cellulose des Ardennes, KNP Leykam in Gratkorn, Condat, Kymmene Nordland etc.

6.4 Corrugated raw materials

The prices of kraftliner, testliner and neutral sulfite semichemical (NSSC) fluting follow each other fairly closely. Kraftliner is usually the price leader due to its quality characteristics. However, recycled fiber prices also have an independent impact on testliner prices.

As with most paper grades, Figure 7 shows that price trends for corrugated raw materials are declining.

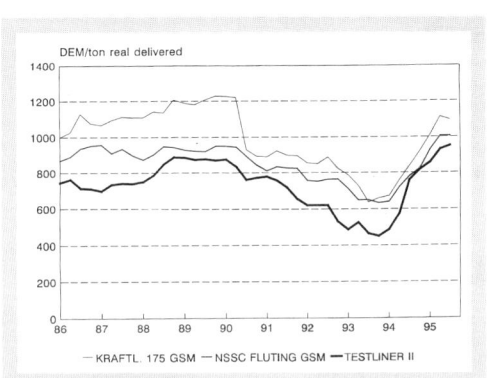

Figure 7. Corrugated board raw material prices in Germany 1986 1995.

World paper markets

6.5 Cartonboards

Figure 8 confirms that FBB and WLC follow each other closely. This is natural, since these grades can replace each other easily in many applications. Price trends are declining slightly. Price fluctuations are less violent than in woodfree grades. This might be due to the fact that there are few FBB producers in Europe and that price discipline is therefore better. Many end users also have special quality requirements. These lower the emphasis on price in the purchase decision.

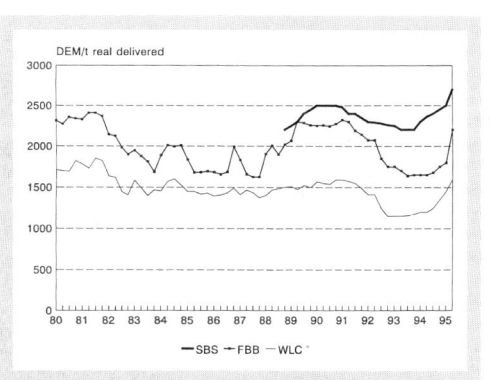

Figure 8. Cartonboard prices in Germany 1980–1995.

6.6 Price stability in Germany 1980–1993

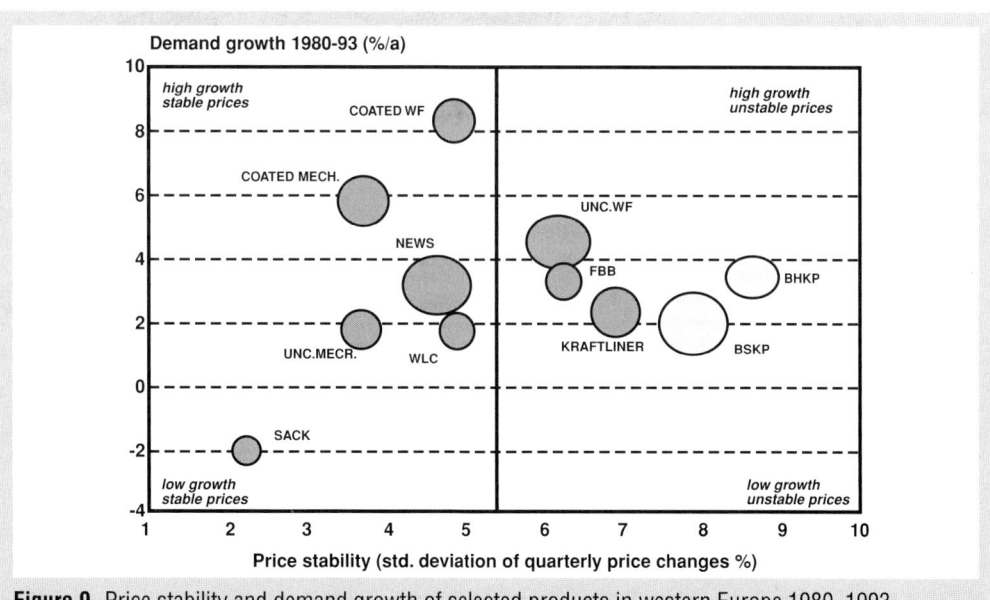

Figure 9. Price stability and demand growth of selected products in western Europe 1980–1993.

Figure 9 measures price stability as a standard deviation of quarterly price changes in percentages on the horizontal axis. The vertical axis shows the growth of demand. The data indicates the following:

1. Pulp and kraftliner have the highest volatility. Besides the price fluctuations caused by demand and supply, it seems that USD exchange variations might increase the fluctuations, as both chemical pulp and kraftliner imports to Germany from the United States are large.
2. Woodfree papers have the second largest volatility. This is natural considering the fact that pulp is the main raw material of these grades.

CHAPTER 5

7 Selection criteria for manufacturing

One key question faces the global forest industry. Which grade or grades can be produced profitably and competitively in a given region? The correct answer to this question is mandatory for success.

The following factors and aspects should be considered and analyzed to find the correct answer:
1. Cost competitiveness
2. Market size and growth potential
3. Quality and availability of raw material
4. Opportunities for further converting
5. Transportation
6. Environmental aspects (permits, legislation, etc.).

Cost competitiveness can be analysed by calculating total manufacturing and transport costs to a given region such as the Ruhr area in Germany or Chicago in the United States for a mill or paper machine and comparing it to its competitors. For bulk products especially, the basic idea is to have lower costs than the competition.

Product price does not influence cost competitiveness. This is a great advantage, as paper prices fluctuate a lot as demonstrated in section 5.6. Exchange rate variation is the greatest uncertainty factor and can change the cost competitiveness drastically in a single day.

One can analyze cost competitiveness for hypothetical new mills. In such an analysis, a new modern mill of similar output and design is located in different regions. The analysis therefore compares the potential cost competitiveness of the chosen locations. Figure 10 shows examples of this kind of analysis.

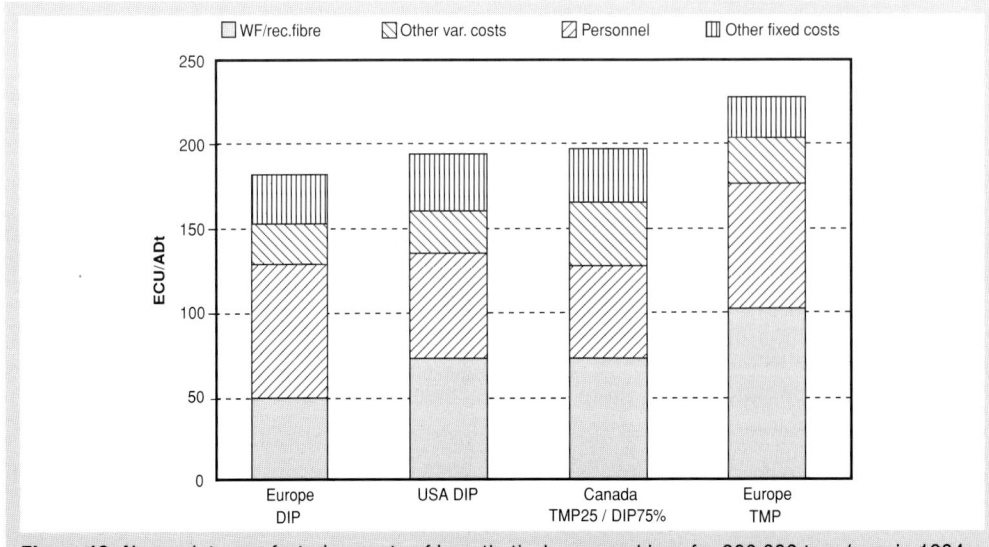

Figure 10. Newsprint manufacturing costs of hypothetical new machines for 300 000 tons/year in 1994.

A model developed by Jaakko Pöyry Consulting Oy can also help analyze the cost competitiveness of existing producers. Analysis of the production costs of each mill or paper machine is reasonably accurate using the published information on mill or paper machine capacity, mill manning, recent investments, etc., with regional unit costs for raw materials, energy, labor, etc. Figure 11 shows an example of this analysis.

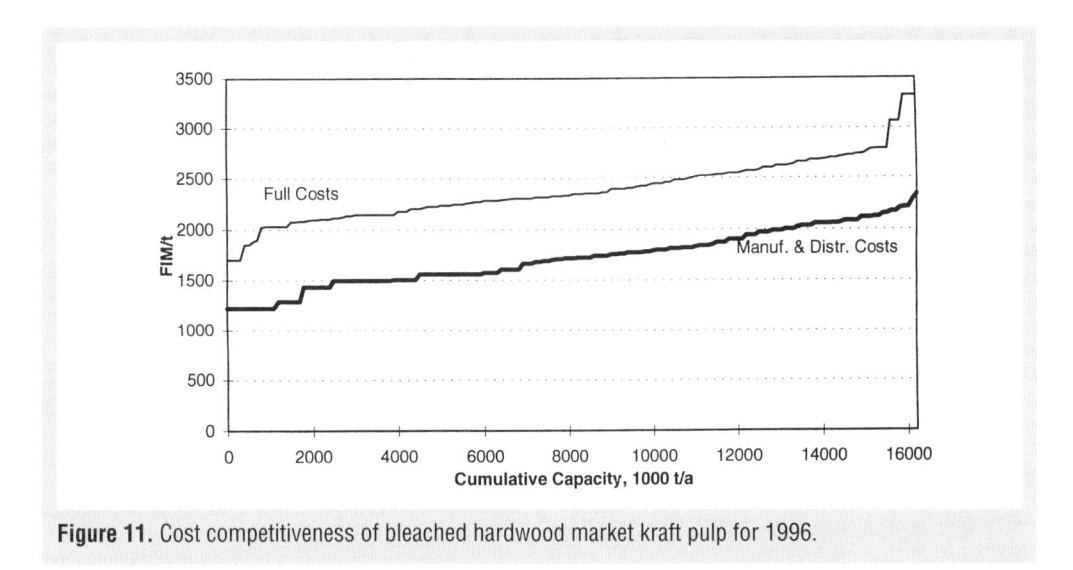

Figure 11. Cost competitiveness of bleached hardwood market kraft pulp for 1996.

Market size and growth potential are important factors. In the case of most bulk products, the unit sizes for new investments have grown so large, 600 000 tons/year for a new pulp mill and 300 000 tons/year for a newsprint machine, that only large and growing markets can absorb the new production without serious price disturbances.

The quality and availability of raw material are also important factors. The large production unit sizes mentioned above require huge amounts of raw materials at reasonable cost. This means that the transportation distances must be kept as short as possible. Suitable quality of the available raw material is naturally important. Practical experience has shown that Scandinavian spruce has superior optical properties in mechanical pulp production for SC and LWC papers. Birch is an excellent material for plywood manufacture and Scandinavian pine for sawn goods. Eucalyptus is an excellent raw material for short fiber chemical pulp, and central European recovered paper is excellent for newsprint manufacture.

Opportunities for further converting are particularly important in a situation where a lack of raw material resources limits the availability of increasing production volumes. In these situations only higher value-added products based on an existing production base can generate growth. Integration benefits are also possible.

Calculation of the ratio of transportation costs to sales price or manufacturing costs allows assessment of transportation. If the transportation is good such as with pulp or kraftliner, the disadvantage of Scandinavian vs. Central European producers is

CHAPTER 5

small. Simultaneously, the advantage of Scandinavian producers vs. North or South American competitors for these grades when delivered to Central Europe decreases.

Environmental aspects have grown to be decisive selection criteria. The length of time required for the necessary permits and the limits for air, noise and water emission etc., are cost factors needing consideration. High standards on environmental issues that can be expensive in the investment phase may later prove to be positive factors through a positive image on main markets.

Table 5 is a summary of the suitability of certain grades from a Scandinavian perspective considering the above criteria. The data in Table 5 should be considered as rough guidelines only.

Table 5. Suitability of main forest industry products for manufacture in Scandinavia.

	Cost competitiveness delivered to Europe	Market size and growth	Availability and quality of raw material	Opportunities for further investment	Transportability	Environmental aspects	General assessment
Sawn goods	-	-	+	+	+	+	Acceptable
Plywood	+	+	++	+	+	+	Good
Particleboard	-	-	-	+	-	+	Bad
Market pulp	-	+	-	++	++	-	Acceptable
Newsprint	+	+	(+)	-	+	+	Acceptable
SC- and LWC-papers	++	++	++	-	+	+	Excellent
Uncoated woodfree	+	+	-	-	+	+	Good
Coated woodfree	+	++	-	-	+	+	Good
Kraftliner	-	-	-	+	++	-	Bad
Corrugated board [1]		+	+	+	+	++	Good
Cartonboards	+	-	-	+	+	+	Acceptable
Liquid packaging board	++	+	-	+	+	-	Good
Tissue [1]		+	+	++	+	+	Good

[1] for local manufacture and delivery

Sources

1   Jaakko Pöyry Consulting Oy

CHAPTER 6

Structure of the global forest industry and main suppliers in the mid 1990s

1	**General**	**77**
2	**Technical structure**	**79**
2.1	Chemical pulp	79
3	**Production structure by grade and region**	**85**
4	**Main suppliers**	**86**
4.1	Total paper and board	86
4.2	Main suppliers by grade	87
5	**Changing industrial structure and concentration**	**91**
5.1	General	91
5.2	Major mergers and acquisitions	92
5.3	Driving forces of mergers and acquisitions	94
6	**Characteristics of major forest industry companies**	**96**
6.1	General	96
6.2	Sales and financial results	97
	Sources	100

Structure of the global forest industry and main suppliers in the mid 1990s

1 General

The global forest industry production of paper and board in 1995 was approximately 260 million tons and that for chemical pulp was approximately 110 million tons. Approximately 9 000 paper machines excluding small paper machines in China and 555 chemical pulp mills produced these volumes. The average production per paper machine was therefore 30 000 tons per year and 195 000 tons per year for a chemical pulp mill. Both these figures are low compared with modern facilities using economy of scale.

To some extent the small unit sizes illustrate the fragmented character that is typical of the forest industry.

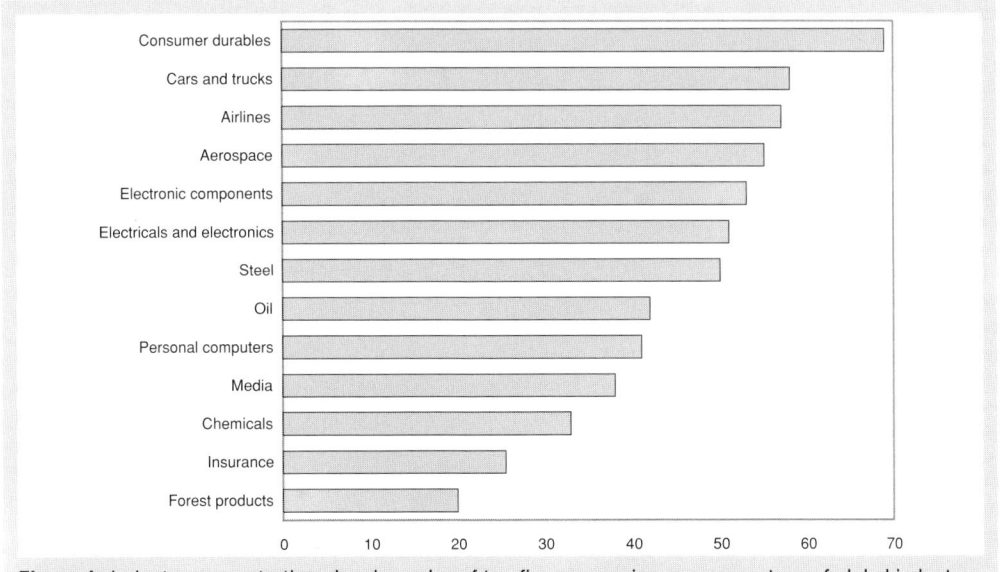

Figure 1. Industry concentration showing sales of top five companies as a percentage of global industry total for 1992.

CHAPTER 6

Figure 1 shows that the top five forest companies in the world had a share of only 20% of total sales in 1992[1]. The corresponding figures for other investment intensive industries such as automobiles, steel, and chemicals were 58%, 50%, and 33%, respectively. The largest forest products company in the world, International Paper, with its annual capacity of 11 million tons had a 4% share of the total global production in 1995. Although concentration has continued steadily since 1992, the same also applies to other branches of the industry. The difference in concentration between the forest industry and other industrial sectors has not declined noticeably.

A new feature influencing the future structure of the forest industry is the emergence of new, fast growing forest products companies in Asia and the Pacific Rim countries. Table 1 shows the biggest companies belonging to this group in the mid 1990s:

Table 1. New forest companies in Asia and the Pacific Rim countries.

Name	Capacity tons/year in early 1996	Location
APP	1.8 million	Indonesia
Hansol	1.6 million	Korea
Cheng Loong	1.4 million	Taiwan

The list of new projects that these and other companies in Asia and the Pacific Rim have announced indicate extremely rapid growth. This growth will influence the forest industry structure globally during the second half of the 1990s and later.

Table 2 illustrates the turbulence in the structures of the twenty largest pulp and paper companies in the world since the mid 1980s[2].

Table 2. Emergence of European pulp and paper super producers.

The effect of the consolidation is obvious as European pulp and paper producers emerge among the world leaders:		
1986	**1990**	**1994**
1 James River	1 International Paper	1 International Paper
2 International Paper	2 James River	2 Nippon Paper
3 Kimberly-Clark	3 Kimberly-Clark	3 Kimberly-Clark / Scott
4 Scott Paper	4 Stone Container	**4 Jefferson Smurfit Group**
5 Champion International	5 Scott Paper	5 New Oji Paper
6 Oji Paper	6 Georgia-Pacific	**6 KNP BT**
7 Weyerhaeuser	7 Champion International	7 James River
8 Georgia-Pacific	8 Great Northern Nekoosa	**8 SCA / PWA**
9 Jujo Paper	9 Weyerhaeuser	9 Stone Container
10 Honshu Paper	10 Oji Paper	**10 Repola / Kymmene**
11 Great Northern Nekoosa	11 Jujo Paper	11 Georgia-Pacific
12 Stone Container	**12 SCA**	**12 Stora**
13 Mead	**13 Stora**	13 Mead
14 Daishowa Paper	14 Honshu Paper	**14 Arjo Wiggins Appleton**
15 Container Corporation	**15 MoDo**	15 Honshu Paper
16 Westvaco	**16 Wiggins Teape Appleton**	16 Champion International
17 Union Camp	**17 Feldmühle**	17 Weyerhaeuser
18 Wiggins Teape	18 Daishowa Paper	**18 Enso-Gutzeit / Veitsiluoto**
19 Boise Cascade	19 Noranda Forest	19 Sappi
20 SCA	20 Boise Cascade	20 Amcor

Since 1986, eight companies have dropped from the top twenty listing. Significantly, in 1986, only two European companies belonged to the top twenty, but in 1994 the figure had increased to seven. Owing to the fragmented nature of the industry, the structural changes experienced during the second half of the 1980s and first half of the 1990s will probably continue. The rate may even increase.

2 Technical structure

2.1 Chemical pulp

In 1995, the world chemical pulp production was approximately 110 million tons produced by 555 pulp mills. Table 3 shows the capacity structure per region[3].

CHAPTER 6

Table 3. Chemical wood pulp mills capacity structure by region for 1996

Capacity 1000 t/a	Finland No. of Mills	Finland (%) Capacity	Sweden No. of Mills	Sweden (%) Capacity	USA No. of Mills	USA (%) Capacity	Canada No. of Mills	Canada (%) Capacity	Brazil No. of Mills	Brazil (%) Capacity	Indonesia No. of Mills	Indonesia (%) Capacity	World total No. of Mills	World total (%) Capacity
-150	1	2	9	9	19	4	7	5	12	9			249	11
150 - 300	4	12	8	25	41	20	24	41	8	33	1	16	141	26
300 - 450	5	26	8	37	40	31	16	43	2	11	2	17	98	30
450 -	8	60	4	29	34	45	3	11	4	47	1	66	67	33
Total	18	100	29	100	134	100	50	100	26	100	2	100	555	100
Total capacity 1000 t/a		6900		7400		46000		13400		5900	6	2400		119000

The data leads to the following conclusions:

1. The 165 largest pulp mills in the 555 total produce almost two-thirds of the total global production.
2. Indonesia and Finland have the most efficient capacity structure. In Indonesia, 83% or 3 mills have a capacity of more than 300 000 tons/year. In Finland, the corresponding figures are 86% or 13 mills.
3. Canada has a weak capacity structure with almost half the capacity or 31 mills below 300 000 tons/year.

2.2 Paper and board

Tables 4–8 show the capacity structures for newsprint, mechanical printing papers, woodfree papers, and corrugated raw materials[3]. Table 8 presents a global summary.

Structure of the global forest industry and main suppliers in the mid 1990s

Table 4. Capacity structure for newsprint machines by region 1996.

Capacity 1000 t/a	Finland No. of PMs	Finland Machine capacity	Finland Grade capacity	Sweden No. of PMs	Sweden Machine capacity	Sweden Grade capacity	Rest of Western Europe No. of PMs	Rest of Western Europe Machine capacity	Rest of Western Europe Grade capacity	USA No. of PMs	USA Machine capacity	USA Grade capacity	Canada No. of PMs	Canada Machine capacity	Canada Grade capacity	World total No. of PMs	World total Machine capacity	World total Grade capacity
-100	3	230	125				15	861	674	4	287	230	27	2106	1987	168	7468	6397
100 - 150	2	220	145	2	245	235	14	1670	1610	18	2306	2031	30	3590	3325	106	12741	11561
150 - 200	3	510	470	2	345	345	8	1335	1275	8	1325	1325	18	3130	3005	59	10030	9725
200 - 250	3	630	510	8	1735	1635	6	1360	1330	12	2670	2670	7	1505	1505	42	9145	8895
250 -	1	250	250	2	540	540	6	1590	1590							12	3195	3195
Total	12	1840	1500	14	2865	2755	49	6816	6479	42	6588	6256	82	10331	9822	387	42579	39773

Table 5. Capacity structure for mechanical printing papers by region 1996.

Capacity 1000 t/a	Finland No. of PMs	Finland Machine capacity	Finland Grade capacity	Sweden No. of PMs	Sweden Machine capacity	Sweden Grade capacity	Rest of Western Europe No. of PMs	Rest of Western Europe Machine capacity	Rest of Western Europe Grade capacity	USA No. of PMs	USA Machine capacity	USA Grade capacity	Canada No. of PMs	Canada Machine capacity	Canada Grade capacity	World total No. of PMs	World total Machine capacity	World total Grade capacity
-100	5	400	275	1	90	90	55	2774	2101	42	2158	1946	32	1709	1537	302	11822	9453
100 - 150	9	1135	1005	5	575	465	20	2359	1809	17	2028	1692	9	1020	810	87	10211	7661
150 - 200	6	1015	875	1	180	180	8	1315	1040	7	1245	1145	5	830	465	32	5405	4145
200 - 250	9	2035	1735	2	440	330	11	2490	2280	5	1045	1045	2	450	450	30	6660	6040
250 -	2	590	590				1	305	305							3	895	895
Total	31	5175	4480	9	1285	1065	95	9243	7535	71	6476	5828	48	4009	3262	454	34993	28194

CHAPTER 6

Table 6. Capacity structure for woodfree papers by region 1996.

Capacity 1000 t/a	Finland No. of PMs	Finland Machine capacity	Finland Grade capacity	Sweden No. of PMs	Sweden Machine capacity	Sweden Grade capacity	Rest of Western Europe No. of PMs	Rest of Western Europe Machine capacity	Rest of Western Europe Grade capacity	USA No. of PMs	USA Machine capacity	USA Grade capacity	Canada No. of PMs	Canada Machine capacity	Canada Grade capacity	World total No. of PMs	World total Machine capacity	World total Grade capacity
-100	10	442	382	17	506	496	376	9025	8094	285	9033	8199	20	726	614	2152	40407	36665
100 - 150	2	230	230	1	100	100	27	3170	3037	26	3052	2870	2	210	210	89	10442	10012
150 - 200	3	540	540	4	625	575	7	1160	1160	18	3045	2580				42	6965	6450
200 - 250	2	410	410	2	430	430	7	1465	1465	9	1950	1950	4	850	850	32	6815	6815
250 -	3	900	900				4	1275	1275	7	1925	1925				15	4350	4350
Total	20	2522	2462	24	1661	1601	421	16095	15031	345	19005	17524	26	1786	1674	2330	68979	64292

Table 7. Capacity structure for corrugated raw materials by region 1996.

Capacity 1000 t/a	Finland No. of PMs	Finland Machine capacity	Finland Grade capacity	Sweden No. of PMs	Sweden Machine capacity	Sweden Grade capacity	Rest of Western Europe No. of PMs	Rest of Western Europe Machine capacity	Rest of Western Europe Grade capacity	USA No. of PMs	USA Machine capacity	USA Grade capacity	Canada No. of PMs	Canada Machine capacity	Canada Grade capacity	World total No. of PMs	World total Machine capacity	World total Grade capacity
-100				4	295	255	235	7279	6702	60	3218	2624	7	435	395	1098	28776	25896
100 - 150							23	2885	2750	24	2828	2653	9	1078	1008	104	12268	11473
150 - 200				2	340	145	11	1810	1565	23	3949	3574	2	300	300	71	11769	10729
200 - 250	2	470	470	2	470	280	11	2440	2370	21	4710	4545	2	420	420	48	10665	10190
250 -	1	300	300	4	1360	1360	3	920	920	49	17108	16873	2	615	615	73	24548	24103
Total	3	770	770	12	2465	2040	283	15334	14307	177	31813	30269	22	2848	2738	1394	88026	82391

Structure of the global forest industry and main suppliers in the mid 1990s

Table 8. Global capacity structure for main paper grades.

Capacity 1000 t/a	Newsprint No. of PMs	Newsprint Capacity distr. (%)	Mechanical PR No. of PMs	Mechanical PR Capacity distr. (%)	Woodfree papers No. of PMs	Woodfree papers Capacity distr. (%)	Corrugated raw materials No. of PMs	Corrugated raw materials Capacity distr. (%)
<100	168	18	302	34	2152	59	1098	33
100 - 150	106	30	87	29	89	15	104	14
150 - 200	59	24	32	15	42	10	71	13
200 - 250	42	21	30	19	32	10	48	12
>250	12	7	3	3	15	6	73	28
Total	387	100	454	100	2330	100	1394	100
Total capacity (1000 t/a)		42 000		35 000		69 000		88 000
Total grade capacity (1000 t/a) [1]		40 000		28 000		64 000		82 000

[1] Estimated capacity allocated to grade concerned

The data in Table 8 forms the basis for the following conclusions:

1. The capacity structure appears to be weakest in fine papers, since approximately 60% of global production capacity consists of paper machines with capacities less than 100 000 tons/year.
2. Large machines produce corrugated raw materials. Machines with annual capacities of 200 000 tons or more form 40% of the global production capacity.

CHAPTER 6

Analysis by grade and region in 1996 leads to the following:
1. Newsprint
   Table 4 shows that Finland and particularly Sweden have a strong capacity structure, since 48% and 79% respectively, of the paper machines in these countries have annual capacities in excess of 200 000 tons/year.
   Despite its position as the largest producer of newsprint, Canada has a weak capacity structure. In that country, 20% of the Canadian capacity (27 paper machines) consists of units smaller than 100 000 tons/year. Only 15% (7 paper machines) consists of machines larger than 200 000 tons/year.
   Western Europe is emerging as a large producer with a healthy capacity structure. In that area, 43% (12 paper machines) of the total production capacity comes from machines with an annual production of over 200 000 tons/year. Only 15% (15 paper machines) consists of machines smaller than 100 000 tons/year.
2. Mechanical printing paper
   Table 5 shows that by far the strongest capacity structure is in Finland, where 51% of the total production capacity (11 paper machines) consists of units with an annual production over 200 000 tons/year and only 8% (5 paper machines) with capacities less than 100 000 tons/year.
   In the United States, only 16% (5 paper machines) of the total production capacity consists of paper machines with production capacities over 200 000 tons/year, and 33% (42 paper machines) have annual capacities smaller than 100 000 tons/year. The Canadian capacity structure is similar to that of the United States, only slightly weaker.
3. Woodfree papers
   Table 6 shows that the weakest structure is in the rest of western Europe where 56% (376 paper machines) of the total production capacity consists of machines smaller than 100 000 tons/year, and only eleven paper machines or 17% have capacities over 200 000 tons/year.
   The United States and Canada have a fairly similar capacity structure compared with the remainder of western Europe.
4. Corrugated raw materials
   Table 7 shows that the United States is definitely the largest producing area. It also has a strong capacity structure, with 69% (70 paper machines) of total production capacity consisting of machines producing more than 200 000 tons/year.

The rest of western Europe is also a large producing area, but its capacity structure is much weaker. Only 22% (or 14 paper machines) of the capacity consists of machines over 200 000 tons/year. In that area, 47% (or 235 paper machines) have capacities smaller than 100 000 tons/year.

3 Production structure by grade and region

Table 9 shows the regional production of paper and board in 1993, and Table 10 shows production by grade[3].

Table 9. Total world production of paper and board by region 1993.

Region	Production of total paper and board Million tons
North America	95.2
Western Europe	66.5
CIS	4.8
Eastern Europe	3.5
Japan	27.8
China	19.5
Other Asia	19.8
Latin America	11.1
Africa	2.6
Oceania	3.0
World total	**253.8**

Table 10. World paper and board production by grade 1993.

Grade	Volume million tons	Share (%)
Newsprint	32.9	13
Printing & writing papers	75.8	30
Industrial paper and board	145.1	57
World total	**253.8**	**100**

The above tables indicate the following:
1. The share of North America and western Europe of the total global production was 162 million tons or approximately 64%.
2. Industrial paper and board grades accounted for the major portion of the total production. This was 145 million tons or 57%.

CHAPTER 6

4 Main suppliers

4.1 Total paper and board

Figure 2 shows the main suppliers of paper and board globally in 1996, and Figure 3 shows the main European suppliers[3].

Figure 2. Main paper and board producers in the world 1996.

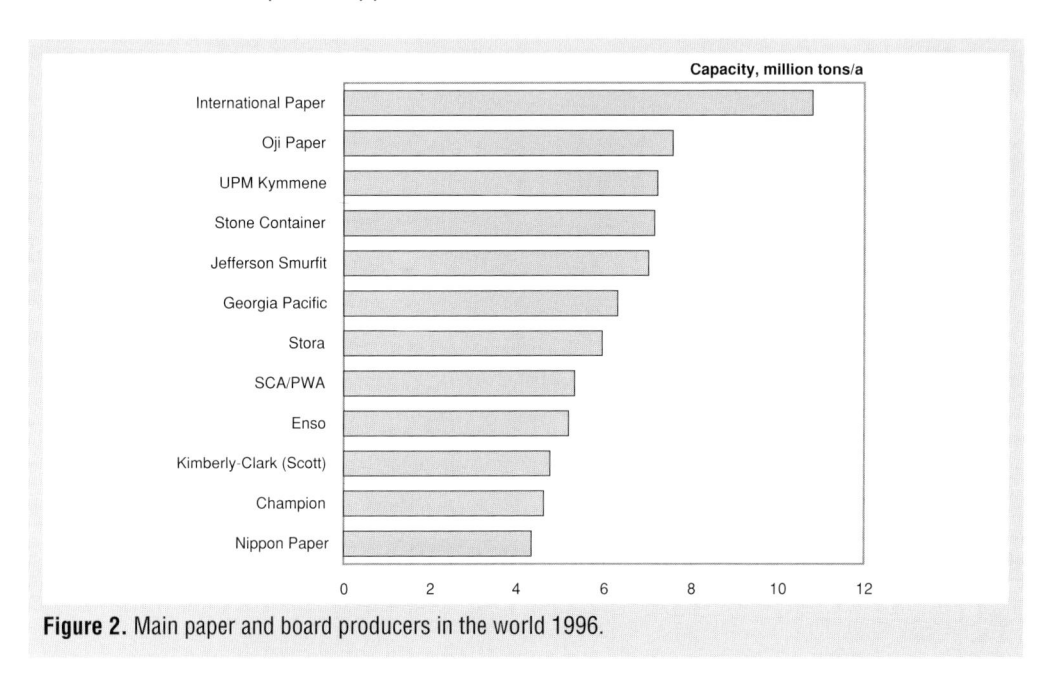

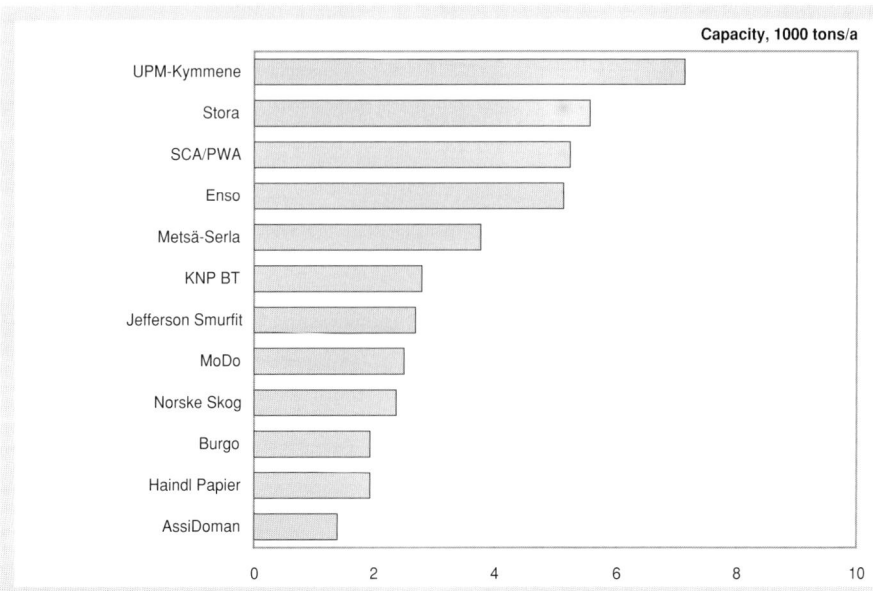

Figure 3. Main paper and board producers in Western Europe 1996.

Structure of the global forest industry and main suppliers in the mid 1990s

Conclusions
1. The five largest suppliers globally are International Paper, Oji Paper, UPM-Kymmene, Stone Container and Jefferson Smurfit. They have a production capacity of 41 million tons/year and a market share of 15%.
2. In Europe, the five largest producers are UPM-Kymmene, Stora, SCA, Enso and Metsä-Serla. They have a combined capacity of 28 million tons/year and a corresponding market share of 40%.

As noted earlier, these figures indicate a high degree of fragmentation in the forest industry.

4.2 Main suppliers by grade

Figures 4–9 show the main suppliers of newsprint, uncoated mechanical papers, coated mechanical papers, uncoated woodfree papers, coated woodfree papers and corrugated raw materials[3]. Table 11 shows the level of global concentration by grade with the market share of the top 5 producers[3].

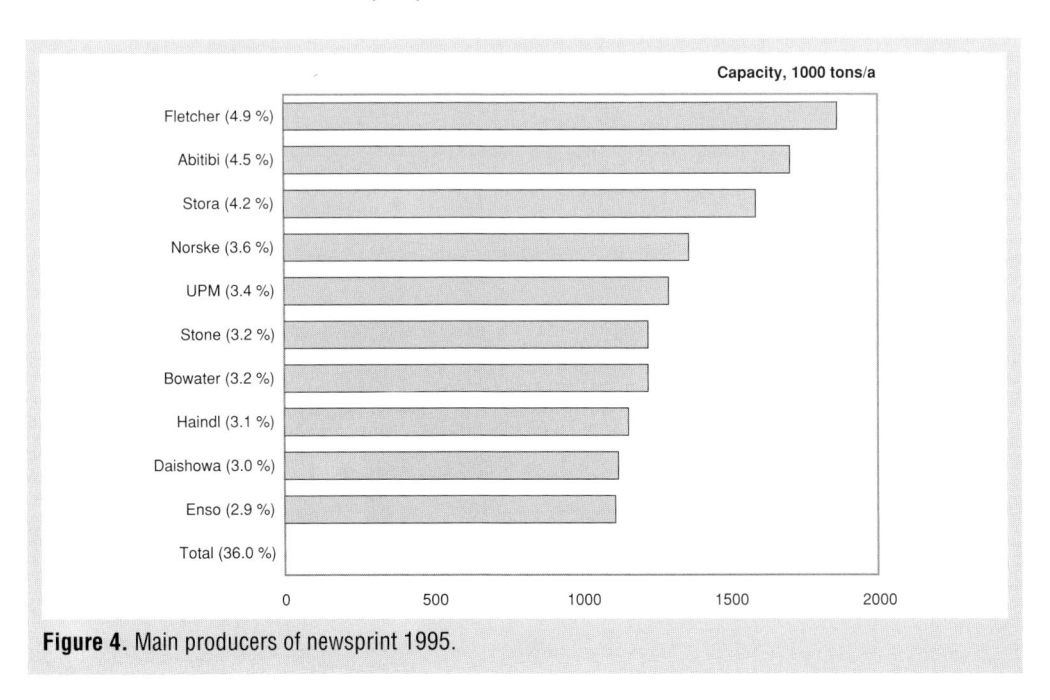

Figure 4. Main producers of newsprint 1995.

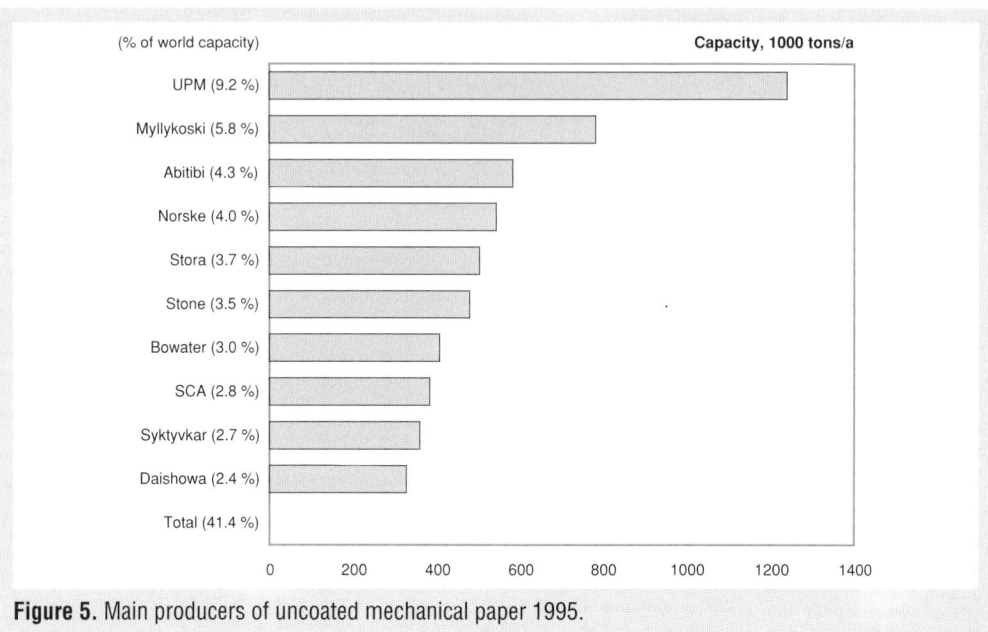

CHAPTER 6

Figure 5. Main producers of uncoated mechanical paper 1995.

Producer	% of world capacity
UPM	9.2 %
Myllykoski	5.8 %
Abitibi	4.3 %
Norske	4.0 %
Stora	3.7 %
Stone	3.5 %
Bowater	3.0 %
SCA	2.8 %
Syktyvkar	2.7 %
Daishowa	2.4 %
Total	41.4 %

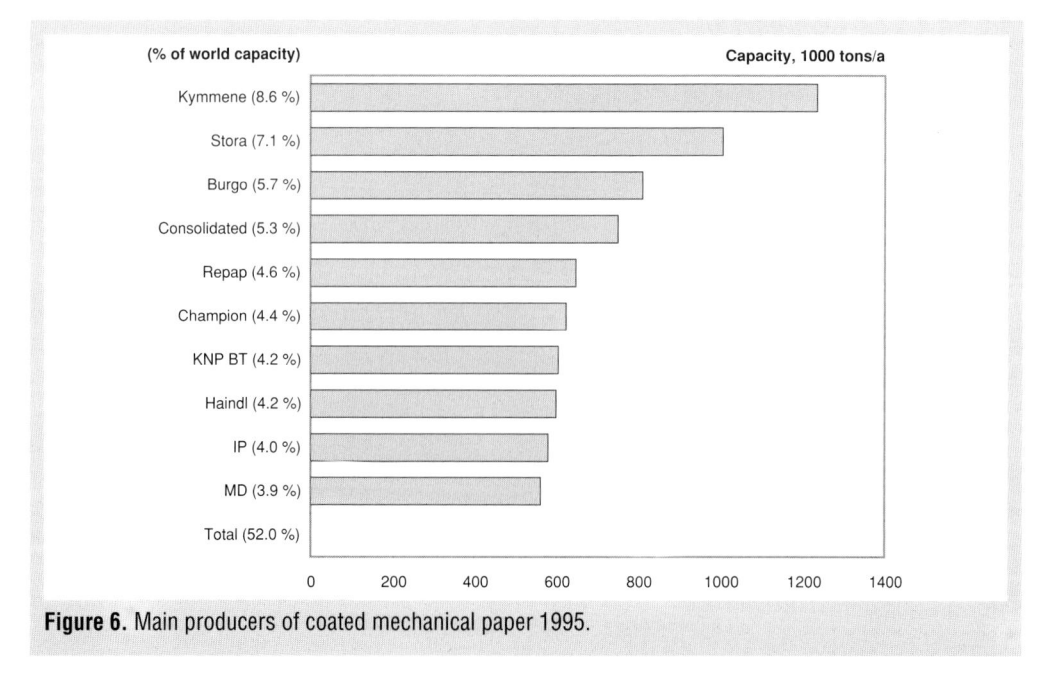

Figure 6. Main producers of coated mechanical paper 1995.

Producer	% of world capacity
Kymmene	8.6 %
Stora	7.1 %
Burgo	5.7 %
Consolidated	5.3 %
Repap	4.6 %
Champion	4.4 %
KNP BT	4.2 %
Haindl	4.2 %
IP	4.0 %
MD	3.9 %
Total	52.0 %

Structure of the global forest industry and main suppliers in the mid 1990s

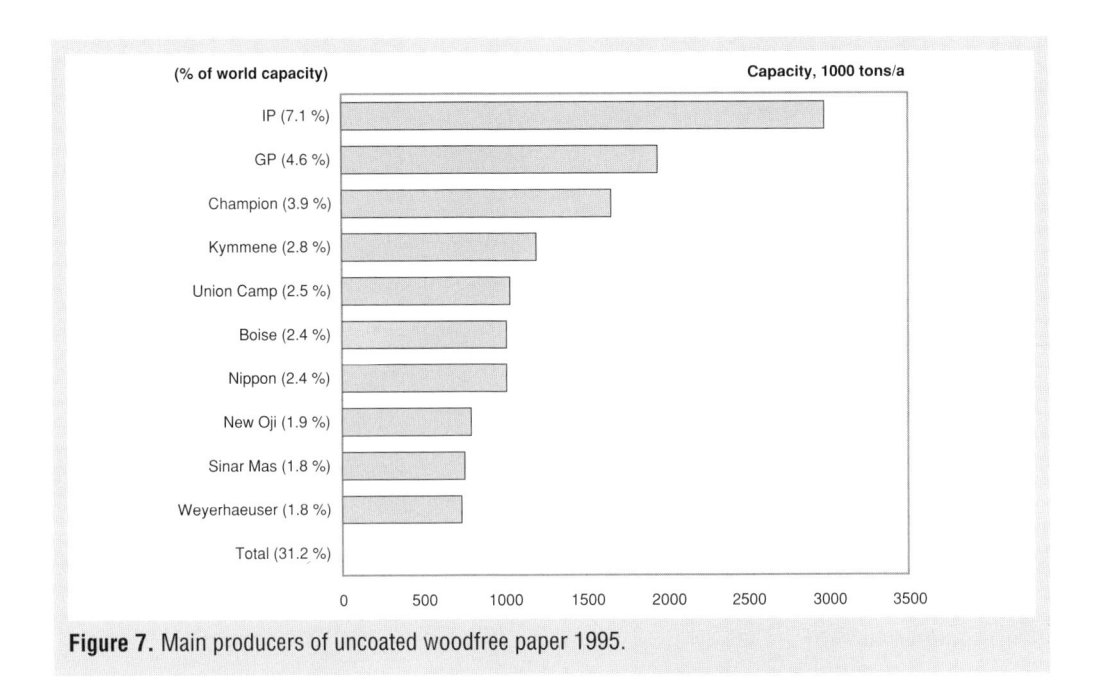

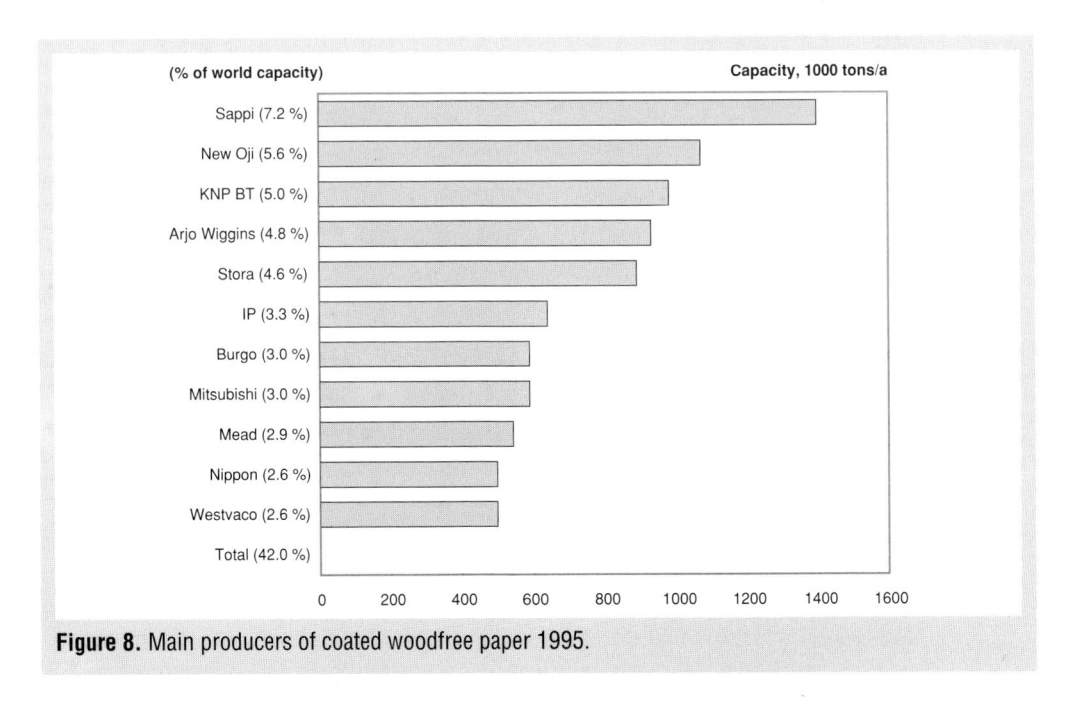

Figure 7. Main producers of uncoated woodfree paper 1995.

Producer	% of world capacity	Capacity, 1000 tons/a
IP	7.1 %	~3000
GP	4.6 %	~1900
Champion	3.9 %	~1600
Kymmene	2.8 %	~1150
Union Camp	2.5 %	~1050
Boise	2.4 %	~1000
Nippon	2.4 %	~1000
New Oji	1.9 %	~800
Sinar Mas	1.8 %	~750
Weyerhaeuser	1.8 %	~750
Total	31.2 %	

Figure 8. Main producers of coated woodfree paper 1995.

Producer	% of world capacity	Capacity, 1000 tons/a
Sappi	7.2 %	~1400
New Oji	5.6 %	~1100
KNP BT	5.0 %	~1000
Arjo Wiggins	4.8 %	~950
Stora	4.6 %	~900
IP	3.3 %	~650
Burgo	3.0 %	~600
Mitsubishi	3.0 %	~600
Mead	2.9 %	~550
Nippon	2.6 %	~500
Westvaco	2.6 %	~500
Total	42.0 %	

CHAPTER 6

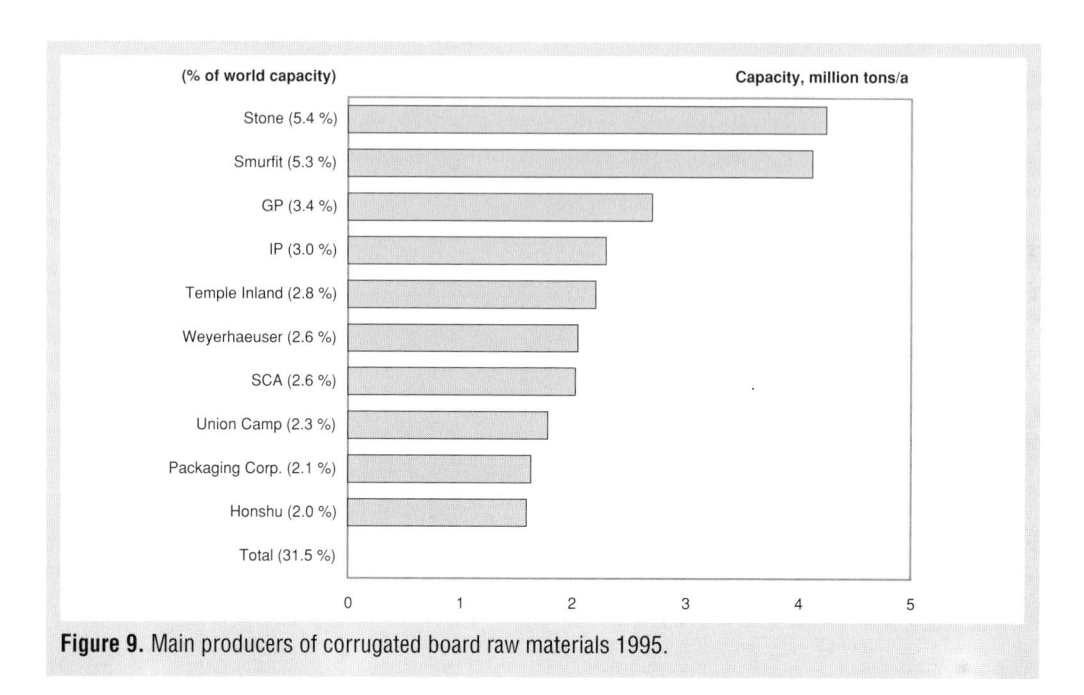

Figure 9. Main producers of corrugated board raw materials 1995.

(% of world capacity) — Capacity, million tons/a

- Stone (5.4 %)
- Smurfit (5.3 %)
- GP (3.4 %)
- IP (3.0 %)
- Temple Inland (2.8 %)
- Weyerhaeuser (2.6 %)
- SCA (2.6 %)
- Union Camp (2.3 %)
- Packaging Corp. (2.1 %)
- Honshu (2.0 %)
- Total (31.5 %)

Table 11. Level of global concentration by grade showing market share of top 5 producers 1995.

	Market share of top 5 producers (%)	Largest producer	Market share of largest producer (%)
Newsprint	21	Fletcher	4.9
Uncoated mechanical papers	27	UPM	9.2
Coated mechanical papers	31	Kymmene	8.6
Uncoated woodfree papers	21	International Paper	7.1
Coated woodfree papers	27	Sappi	7.2
Corrugated raw materials	20	Stone	5.4

The above data indicates two main conclusions where level of concentration is concerned:
1. The leading producer's market share is under 10% for all grades.
2. The total market share of the top five producers varies between 20% and 30% for all grades.
   This clearly demonstrates that in paper and board markets any discipline to stabilize the markets exercised by large suppliers is neither realistic nor possible. Free competition and pricing based on market forces are dominant.

Structure of the global forest industry and main suppliers in the mid 1990s

5 Changing industrial structure and concentration

5.1 General

Despite the fact that the forest industry is fragmented, important and significant changes have taken place particularly since the mid 1980s. The key factor has been concentration through mergers and acquisitions.

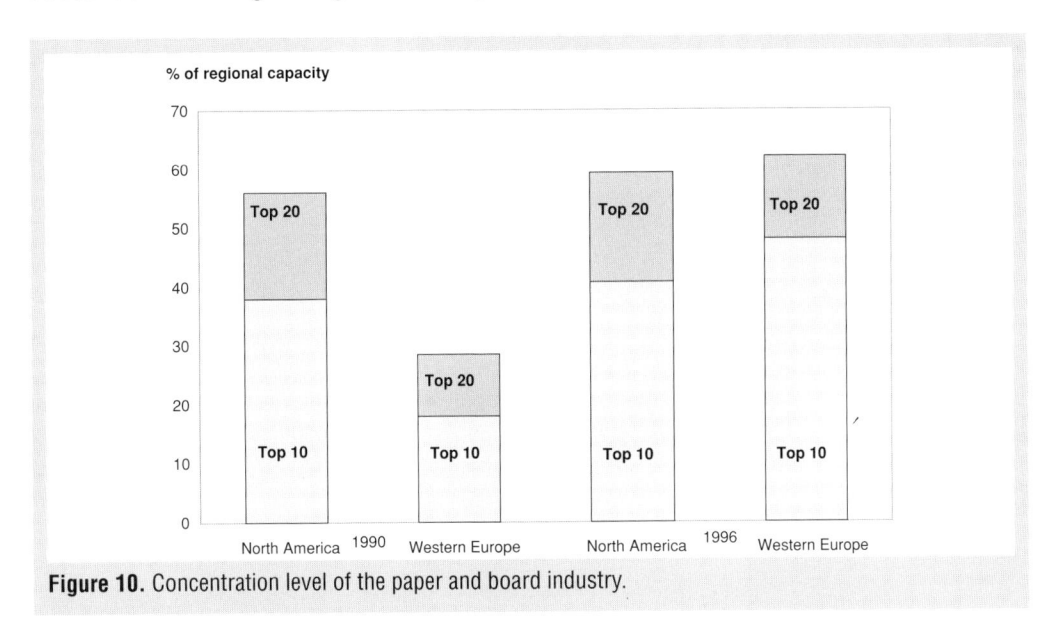

Figure 10. Concentration level of the paper and board industry.

Figure 10 shows the share of regional capacity of the top ten and twenty producers in North America and western Europe in 1980 and 1996[3]. The level of concentration in North America has been fairly constant with the market share of the top ten producers around 40%. The share of the top ten producers in western Europe has increased from less than 20% in 1980 to almost 50% in 1996. As a result of this development the largest companies in Europe have grown much faster than the largest companies in North America.

Table 12. Expansion of the top 30 North American and European pulp and paper companies 1980–1993.

Ranking	Europe Sales in USD Billion 1980	Europe Sales in USD Billion 1993	Growth t/a	North America Sales in USD Billion 1980	North America Sales in USD Billion 1993	Growth t/a
1 - 10	10.0	35.0	10.5	30	70	6.8
11 - 20	4.9	12.0	7.1	6	21	4.7
21 - 30	2.5	4.7	5.0	5	10	5.4

CHAPTER 6

Table 12 illustrates this situation and also explains the reasons for the changes in the global top twenty list of large companies with so many European companies entering and North American companies exiting this list.

5.2 Major mergers and acquisitions

Figure 11 illustrates the merger and acquisition activity in 1975–1994 among the top 100 companies in the global forest industry[2]. The average number of such events in 1975–1985 was 10–20, but during 1990–1995 the corresponding figure was doubled at 30–40. The values involved in the global merger and acquisition activities have a similar trend as Figure 12 shows[4].

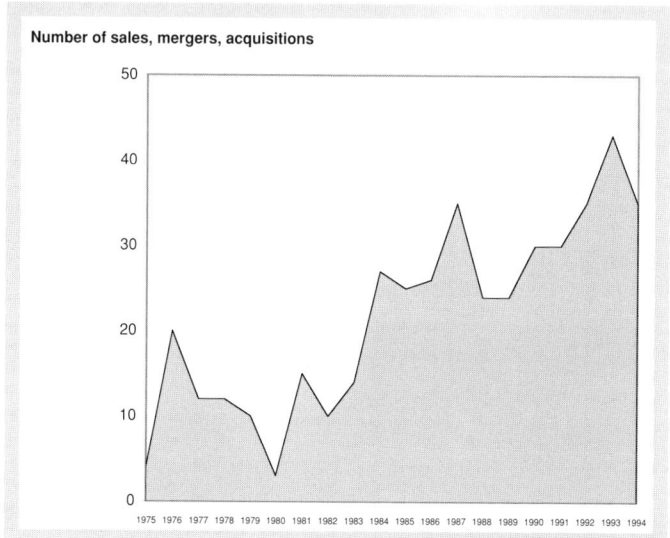

Figure 11. Merger activity among top 100 global pulp, paper and board companies 1975–1994.

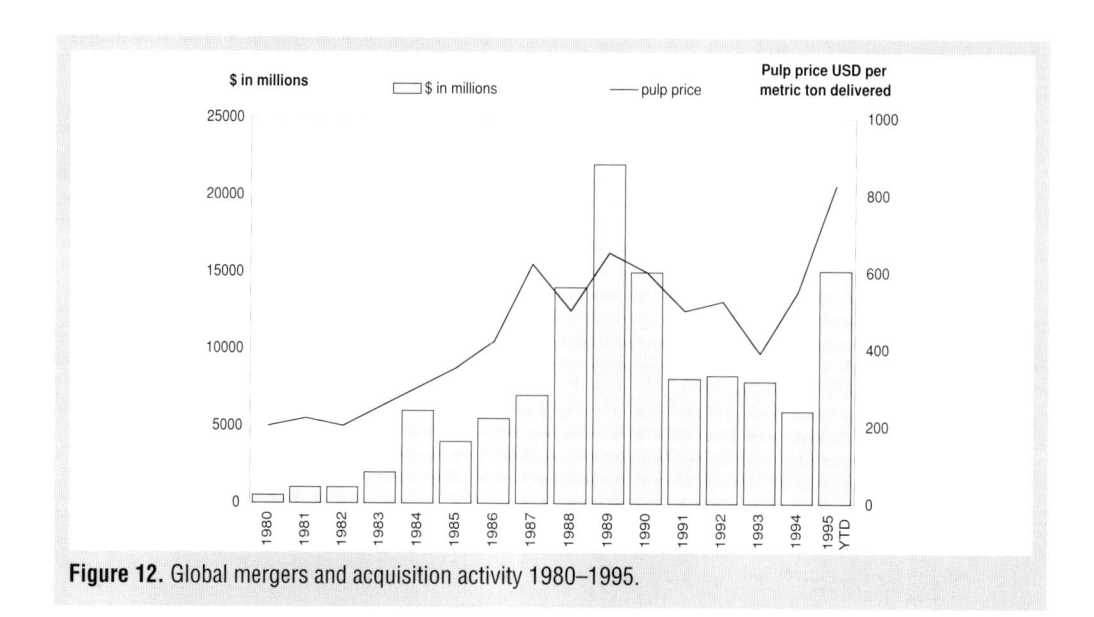

Figure 12. Global mergers and acquisition activity 1980–1995.

Structure of the global forest industry and main suppliers in the mid 1990s

A peak was reached in 1988–1990 with activities worth USD 15–23 billion/year. A similar peak occurred in 1995. During the years 1991–1994, the values involved in the merger and acquisition activities were USD 7–8 billion/year. It is interesting that the values of merger and acquisition activities have closely followed the market pulp price. This indicates the close relationship of good earnings with merger activity.

Table 13. Mergers and acquisitions in Europe 1985–1996.

MERGERS & ACQUISITIONS IN EUROPE 1985–1996
1. FINLAND
1.1 Enso - Varkaus - Tervakoski - Berghuizer - Tampella Forest - Veitsiluoto
1.2 Kaukas - Kymmene - Schauman - Chapelle - UPM
1.3 Metsäliitto - Serlachius - Kemi - Holmen Hygien - Myllykoski - München - Dachau - Kyro - Biberist
1.4 Rauma - Repola - Rosenlew - UPM - Joutseno - Kajaani
1.5 Veitsiluoto - Oulu
2. SWEDEN
2.1 Stora - Billerud - Papyrus - Forenede - Swedish Match - Feldmühle - Begin
2.2 SCA - Lilla Edet - Laakirchen - Reedpack - PWA - (Mondi)
2.3 MoDo - Iggesund - Holmens - Fiskeby - Thames Board - Alicel / Alipap
3. NORWAY
3.1 Norske Skog - Union - Follum - Tofte - Saugbruksföreningen - KNP/Bruck
4. CONTINENTAL EUROPE
4.1 Haindl - Parenco - Steyermühl
4.2 Mondi - Frantschach - Neusiedler - Pöls - Aylesford
4.3 BT - KNP - VRG - Leykam
4.4 Arjomari - Wiggins Teape - Appleton
4.5 IP - Aussedat Rey - Zanders - Kvidzyn - Federal - Thomas Tait
4.6 Federal - Thomas Tait
4.7 Burgo - Cellulose des Ardennes
4.8 Fletcher - UK Paper
4.9 Manville - Fiskeby Board
4.10 Sappi - Star - Hannover Papier
4.11 Jefferson Smurfit - Cellulose du Pin
4.12 James River - Kaysersberg - Sarrio - Various others
4.13 Scott Paper - Feldmühle Tissue

Table 13 shows the mergers and acquistions in Europe during 1985–1996.

CHAPTER 6

Finland

At the beginning of the 1980s, Finland had more than twenty independent forest companies. In 1996, there were three major companies remaining: UPM-Kymmene, Enso and Metsä-Serla – Myllykoski.

Sweden

The main merger and acquisition activities by Swedish forest companies resulted in five major forest companies remaining in 1996 – Stora, SCA, MoDo, Assi and Södra.

Norway

Norske Skog has since 1985 merged practically all other main producers in Norway including Union, Tofte, Follum and Saugbruksföreningen.

Continental Europe

Since 1985, Continental Europe has experienced two main types of mergers and acquisitions. The first have been internal mergers and acquisitions of continental European producers. The second type came from Scandinavian or overseas companies entering central Europe. Typical mergers and acquisitions belonging to the first group were Arjomari with Wiggins Teape, KNP with Leykam, Jefferson Smurfit with Cellulose du Pin and Burgo with Cellulose des Ardennes.

Mergers and acquisitions initiated by Scandinavian producers were numerous. The driving force in these cases was the need to be closer to major markets and customers as well as to recycled fiber sources. Table 13 shows that Swedish companies acquired central European companies, while Finnish companies focused on building new mills. As examples, UPM built Shotton and Stracel and Kymmene built Caledonia and Nordland.

Mergers and acquisitions initiated by overseas producers were caused by the same reasons as those by the Scandinavian companies. The largest paper company in the world, International Paper, has been particularly active as have the South African companies Mondi and Sappi.

5.3 Driving forces of mergers and acquisitions

As Figures 11 and 12 have shown, merger and acquisition activity increased significantly after 1985. The main reasons were the following:
1. The growth of the importance of recycled fiber as a raw material for the paper industry, especially for newsprint, as the use of deinked pulp (DIP) gained momentum. Recycled fiber was not only ecologically feasible, it was also cost competitive. Scandinavian producers had only limited access to this raw material domestically. Acquisition of central European companies close to densely populated regions and recycled fiber resources was therefore a good way to access this resource.

Structure of the global forest industry and main suppliers in the mid 1990s

2. Economy of scale increased the size of new pulp and paper mills dramatically. Despite this, the investment per unit output did not decrease. Figure 13 shows that this factor actually remained constant causing the absolute investment to reach levels not experienced earlier[3].

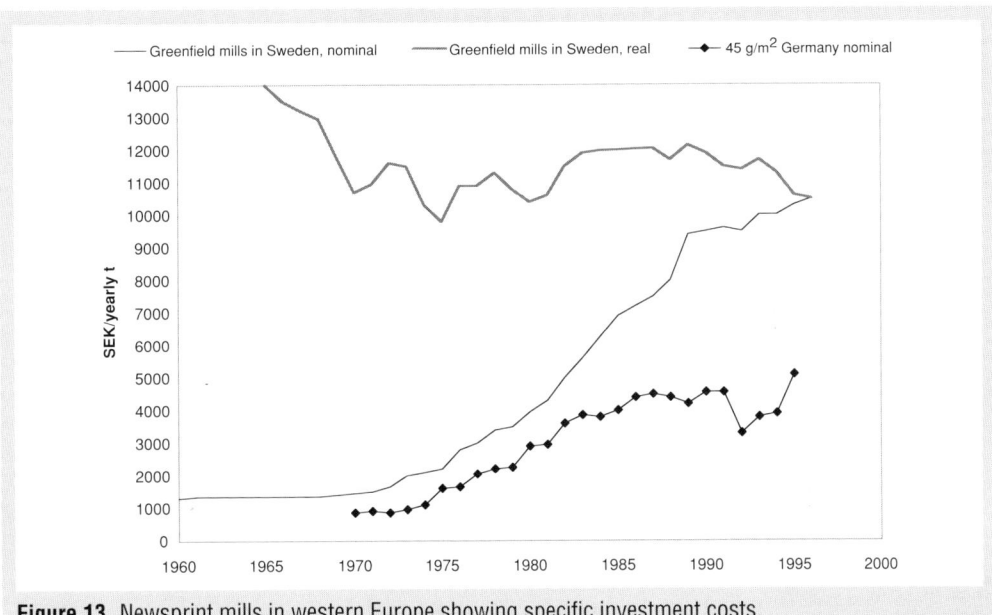

Figure 13. Newsprint mills in western Europe showing specific investment costs.

Many companies of small and medium size were therefore in a situation where a USD 500 million investment generated a risk too high for them. Simultaneously, most product price trends declined 0.5–1.0%/year in real terms. This made it necessary to use all available competition factors to the utmost to safeguard profitability including economy of scale. Declining margins did not allow building new pulp and paper mills of small to medium size any longer. In this situation, an opportunity to merge with a large company was the only feasible alternative for a producer of small to medium size.

3. The cyclical nature of many product prices such as pulp and newsprint was slight from 1960 to the mid 1970s. Since then, the cyclical nature has become part of the daily life of the forest industry. Prices have varied violently. Market pulp was USD 1000/ton in October 1995 and USD 500/ton in May 1996. The speed of the changes has also increased radically. Prediction of cycles has therefore become ever more uncertain and risks have increased. This became a proven fact during the early 1990s when six of eight new fine paper machines in Europe changed hands due to financial crises caused by an unexpected decrease in prices. This environment requires large unit sizes and strong balance sheets to survive. These are two factors that small companies lack. Mergers have been a way to lower these risks.

4. The desire to gain a larger market share quickly without adding new capacity has also been an important motive. The Swedish companies especially have practiced this strategy by directing approximately half their investments in mergers and acquisitions during 1985–1995. These companies have simultaneously gained marketing networks and market intelligence that have further strengthened their overall position.
5. The concentration of the customer base – particularly in newsprint and magazine publishing – caused buyers to grow enormously. International publishers wanted to buy large amounts of paper from a limited number of suppliers. In addition, ensuring safety of supplies under all circumstances was necessary. Only large suppliers having many supply locations in different countries could guarantee this requirement. The ability to supply large amounts of publishing papers from different locations became a prerequisite which further contributed to merger and acquisition activity.

The fragmented structure of the pulp and paper industry still calls for more consolidation through mergers and acquisitions. Some actions have failed partly or totally such as SCA and MoDo in 1994. A more concentrated industry is also a necessity for the pulp and paper industry in the future, if this industrial sector wants to compare favorably to other industrial segments.

6 Characteristics of major forest industry companies

6.1 General

Figure 2 shows the twelve largest forest industry companies measured by paper and board production volumes for 1996. International Paper is definitely the largest with a total production capacity of 11 million tons/year, followed by Oji Paper with 7.5 million tons/year. The smallest of the twelve companies is Nippon Paper with 4.5 million tons/year production capacity.

For Europe, Figure 3 shows that UPM-Kymmene is the leader with 7 million tons/year production capacity. Three other companies – Stora, SCA and Enso – exceed the 4 million tons/year figure.

In the European league all the main producers have participated actively in mergers and acquisitions as Table 13 shows. This technique has therefore often been the driving force for growth.

6.2 Sales and financial results

Table 15 shows a comparison of sales growth, profitability and investments of the largest producers in Europe and North America listed in Table 14 for 1986–1995.

Table 14. Largest producers in Europe and North America.

COMPANIES
Metsä-Serla
Enso-Gutzeit, Enso
Kymmene
UPM, UPM-Kymmene
MoDo
Stora
SCA
Södra
Georgia-Pacific
International Paper
Weyerhauser
Kimberly-Clark
James River
Champion International
Mead

COMPANIES
Avenor
Abitibi-Price
Domtar
Repap
Cascades
MacMillan Bloedel
Noranda Forest
KNP BT
PWA
Haindl
Arjo Wiggins Appleton

Table 15. Comparison of sales growth, profitability and investments of largest producers 1986–1995.

1986-1995	Finland	Sweden	USA	Canada	Central Europe
1.) Aggregate Sales Growth (%/a)	13.6	18.5	6.9	4.5	13.5
2.) Aggregate Deflated Sales Growth (%/a)	10.3	13.1	4.4	1.6	10.9
3.) Average ROCE (%)	8.6	10.3	11.4	7.0	9.9
4.) Average ROE (%)	6.9	10.0	10.9	5.1	10.5
5.) Average Capital Turnover	0.80	1.14	1.23	1.17	1.74
6.) Total Investments / Sales (%)	18.7	17.0	10.9	10.6	9.3
7.) Average EBIT / Sales (%)	10.8	9.0	9.2	6.0	5.7

The following are significant comments regarding the above data:
1. European companies have grown significantly faster than their North American counterparts. The deflated sales growth in Canada has been particularly slow at an annual average of 1.6%.
2. Profitability measured by return on capital employed (ROCE) has been highest in the United States at 11.4% followed by Sweden at 10.3% and central

CHAPTER 6

Europe with 9.9%. Finland and Canada have clearly been at lower levels of 8.6% and 7.0%, respectively.

Measured by return on equity (ROE), Sweden, the United States, and central Europe have all exceeded 10%. Finland and Canada have been significantly lower at 6.9% and 5.1% respectively.

Measured by earnings before interest and taxes (EBIT)/Sales the 10.8% figure for Finland is the highest, followed by the United States at 9.2% and Sweden at 9.0%. Canada and central Europe are at a lower level with 6.0% and 5.7% respectively.

3. Total investments have been highest in Finland and Sweden with 18.7% and 17.0%, respectively. The United States, Canada and central Europe have all been at approximately the same level of 10%. These differences are significant, and they indicate a clear difference in investment strategy.
4. There are also big differences in capital turnover. The fastest turnover rate is in central Europe with 1.74. Sweden, the United States, and Canada are at approximately 1.2. The turnover rate in Finland is very low at 0.8.

The span for the statistics in Table 15 is ten years. This evens random fluctuations. The following conclusions result from the data:

1. Finland

   The high investment rate has resulted in a high EBIT figure and fast sales growth. Investments in new machinery and equipment, rather than mergers and acquisitions have caused the low capital turnover rate. Considering the average risk-free rate of capital during 1986–1995 at approximately 10–12%, ROCE and ROE have been unsatisfactory. ROCE should have been approximately 12–14% and ROE 18–20%.

2. Sweden

   The investment rate in Sweden has been roughly the same as in Finland. EBIT level has been lower, but sales growth has been higher. These factors combined with high capital turnover indicate that Swedish companies have invested more in mergers and acquistions than in new machinery. The Swedish investment strategy has been different compared with Finnish strategies.

There is an explanation for these conclusions.

When buying existing mills or companies, the sales from these acquisitions combine with that of the parent company the day after closing the deal. With new investments, no sales are generated for 18–24 months after the investment decision. It usually takes 1–2 years after startup before full production and sales levels are reached. This lowers sales growth compared with mergers. It particularly lowers capital turnover, since capital employed increases but sales growth lags by 2–3 years.

Existing mills and companies are seldom as modern and efficient as new machinery. This explains the lower EBIT figures for Sweden.

Structure of the global forest industry and main suppliers in the mid 1990s

3. United States
   The investment rate has been at a lower level compared with Finland and Sweden. This has caused sales growth to be less than half that of Scandinavian producers. The EBIT level has been almost as high as in Scandinavia.
4. Canada
   Investment rate has been on the same level as in the United States, but both sales growth and EBIT levels are lower. This implies inefficient use of investment funds. The low profitability figures – ROCE and ROE – further substantiate this.
5. Central Europe
   The investment rate is on the same level as the United States and Canada. EBIT levels have been low, but sales growth and capital turnover were high. One explanation for this is the fact that KNP BT, AWA and to some extent PWA have large merchanting operations that operate on low EBIT level but high capital turnover due to lower capital requirements in the merchant business.

CHAPTER 6

Sources

1. *International Data Corp., Morgan Stanley, Jaakko Pöyry Consulting Oy*
2. *Pulp and Paper International (PPI)*
3. *Jaakko Pöyry Consulting Oy*
4. *Merrill Lynch*

CHAPTER 7

Cost structure and management accounting

1	**Income statement and balance sheet**	**102**
1.1	Introduction	102
1.2	Definitions	102
2	**Profitability**	**104**
3	**Shareholder value**	**108**
3.1	General	108
3.2	EVA as a concept	109
3.3	EVA and the market value of a company	110
3.4	Value based management	110
4	**Investment behavior in certain countries**	**111**
5	**Appropriate investment levels**	**113**
6	**Management accounting**	**114**
7	**Comparison of order profitability**	**117**
8	**Factors affecting production rate**	**119**
9	**Evaluation of development investment**	**122**
10	**Distribution of economic information to the operating floor**	**124**
	Sources	125

CHAPTER 7

Cost structure and management accounting

1 Income statement and balance sheet

1.1 Introduction

Two concepts for evaluating the economic results and status of a company are the income statement and balance sheet. The purpose of the income statement is to describe the economic performance and operating results for a certain period that is usually one year. Stock listed companies usually also publish unaudited income statements three or four times a year, on a tertiary or quarterly basis. The balance sheet shows the financial position of the company at the end of a certain accounting period.

1.2 Definitions

Table 1 provides an example of an income statement, balance sheet and sources of funds.

Table 1. Income statement and balance sheet.

Income statement		Sources and application of funds	
Sales	100	EBIT	17
Cost of goods sold		Depreciation	6
- raw materials, energy	-43	Financial income and expenses	-5
- outside services, rents, personnel	-34	Taxes	-1
EBITD	23	Change in working capital	-10
Depreciation according to plan	-6	Cash flow from operations	7
EBIT	17		
Financial income + expenses	-5	Investments	-5
Profit after financing items	12	Cash flow before financing	2
Taxes	-1		
Net profit	11	Financing	
		Decrease in loans	2
		Balance	0
Balance sheet			
Assets		Liabilities	
Fixed assets		Shareholders' equity	
- intangible assets	1	- non-distributable equity	27
- tangible assets	89	- distributable equity+retained profits	13
- financial assets	13	Reserves	20
Current assets		Long-term and current liabilities	
- investments	15	- long-term	59
- receivables	17	- current	23
- cash	7		
	142		142

Cost structure and management accounting

The following definitions and explanations are important (Table 2):
1. Sales
   The flow of money into the company comes mainly from sales or turnover. Sales calculations use the following formula: volume of goods sold x unit price free delivered to a customer's location. Until 1994, sales calculations in Finland used the formula: volume of goods sold x unit price at mill. This inflated sales figures but deflated relative profitability figures such as EBIT in relation to sales compared with earlier years.
   Sales are often a measure of the size of a company.
2. Gross profit or gross margin
   The gross profit or earnings before interest, taxes and depreciation (EBITD) indicates how much remains to cover necessary investments, payments to money lenders as interest and amortization of debts, payments to the state as taxes, and to the shareholders as dividends. Gross margin is EBITD divided by sales.
3. Free cash flow
   Free cash flow from operations is the gross profit (EBITD) less capital expenditure, taxes plus/minus the change in working capital.
   Free cash flow can be used for three purposes:
   - repayment of debt
   - repayment of interest
   - payments of dividends.
   Evaluation methods such as depreciation do not influence free cash flow. It is therefore an exact figure. On the other hand, changes in working capital often have a great impact on cash flow. In the example of Table 1, the increase of working capital was double the total investments. Working capital has a cost element in the form of interest costs. Great emphasis is therefore necessary to monitor and control working capital.
4. Investments
   Investments fall into several different categories:
   (i) Replacement investments that are necessary to maintain the production capacity, efficiency and quality of operation in the medium and long term. Replacement investments do not usually have any profitability. Differentiating between replacement investments and maintenance costs is difficult. From a practical point of view, replacement investments and maintenance costs are usually of the same nature. Drastic curtailment of the replacement investment level usually causes maintenance costs to increase.

(ii) Development investments improve the earning potential and performance of a mill, paper machine or pulp mill. Profitability as pay back is usually the most important decision criterion.

(iii) Strategic investments significantly improve the earning capacity of the entire company, change its production structure, or both.

Because development and strategic investments increase earnings, increasing the company's indebtedness may partly finance them. Future earnings then pay interest and amortization.

5. Depreciation

Depreciation is cost that should cover the wear and tear of an investment made earlier by allocating the investment costs over the useful life of the assets. Depreciation is a bookkeeping transaction. It is not a cash item. When a certain depreciation is made in the income statement, a similar reduction is made in the balance sheet on item fixed assets. Theoretically, a mill should be able to reinvest a sum at least equal to the depreciation from its operative cash flow to remain competitive. Loans to finance replacement investments weaken the financial position of a company, since its indebtedness increases without a commensurate increase in earning potential.

Depreciation rules between countries still differ. This fact is important when comparing companies from different countries.

6. Operating profit or operating margin

The operating profit or EBIT is defined as earnings before interest and taxes. Operating margin is operating profit (EBIT) divided by sales. This is a good measure of a company's financial performance.

2 Profitability

Table 1 shows the balance sheet of a fictional company. Calculation of certain indexes is possible using this balance sheet. Since availability of capital is often considered the restricting factor for expansion, many profitability indexes measure the return of capital in one form or another. The following indexes are most commonly used.

$$\text{Return on capital employed} = \frac{\text{Result}}{\text{Capital employed}} \tag{1}$$

Calculation of the return can use total capital employed or equity. When calculating return on total capital employed, the result should be EBIT from the income statement. The effects of depreciation have been deducted, since these are comparable to maintenance costs and should therefore not be included in the result. Capital employed in principle is the sum of fixed assets plus working capital.

Cost structure and management accounting

Calculation on return on capital employed therefore uses the following equation:

$$\text{Return on capital employed ROCE} = \frac{\text{EBIT}}{\text{Capital employed}} = \frac{\text{EBITD} - \text{depreciation}}{\text{Capital employed}} \quad (2)$$

When calculating return on equity, interest costs on debt must be deducted from EBIT and debt deducted from total assets as follows:

$$\text{Return on equity ROE} = \frac{\text{EBITD} - \text{depreciation} - \text{net interest} - \text{taxes}}{\text{Total assets} - \text{debt}} \quad (3)$$

$$= \frac{\text{EBIT} - \text{net interest} - \text{taxes}}{\text{Total assets} - \text{debt}}$$

Calculation of return on capital employed can also use the following formula:

$$\text{Return on capital employed} = \frac{\text{Result}}{\text{Capital employed}}$$

$$= \frac{\text{Result}}{\text{Sales}} \times \frac{\text{Sales}}{\text{Capital employed}} = \frac{\text{EBIT}}{\text{Sales}} \times \frac{\text{Sales}}{\text{Capital employed}} \quad (4)$$

In the above formula, return on capital has two components – operating margin or EBIT divided by sales and capital turnover. The first provides the margin of sales, and the second shows how quickly capital rotates compared with total capital employed.

In addition to these basic measurements, a number of indexes are useful for balance sheet analyses. Simplified forms for some commonly used formulas follow:

$$\text{Gearing} = 100 \times \frac{\text{Net interest bearing liabilities}}{\text{Equity}} \quad (5)$$

Gearing is a measure of capital structure. This is indebtedness compared with equity. The figure should normally be below 100. For companies with a strong balance sheet, it is approximately 50.

$$\text{Earning per share EPS} = \frac{\text{Result}}{\text{Number of shares}} \quad (6)$$

CHAPTER 7

EPS is a measure of the results per share. It provides a common calculation using the current share price. The following formula shows the price earning ratio (PE-ratio):

$$\text{Price earning ratio PE-ratio} = 100 \times \frac{\text{Share price at stock exchange}}{\text{EPS}} \quad (7)$$

The PE-ratio is usually 5–20 but can vary outside this range. A high PE-ratio means higher expectations on the stock market that share prices, dividends, or both will increase due to a favorable outlook and results for the company.

$$\text{Market capitalization} = \text{Number of shares} \times \text{current share price at stock exhange} \quad (8)$$

Table 2 gives a detailed and accurate list of indexes computable from balance sheets.

Table 2. Definitions of certain financial factors and ratios.

EBITD	= Gross profit	= Earnings before interest, taxes and depreciation
EBITD/Sales	= Gross margin	
EBIT	= Operating profit	= Earnings before interest and taxes
EBIT/Sales	= Operating margin	
EPS	= Earnings per share	
Enterprise value	= Market value + interest bearing net debt	
Equity ratio	= Book value of equity / Total assets	
Free cash flow	= EBITD - taxes - investment +/- change in working capital	
Gearing	= Interest bearing net debt/book value of equity, or debt/equity ratio	
Market capitalization or market value	= Number of shares x present share price or market value	
Net profit	= EBIT - interest costs - taxes	
NPV	= Net present value of future cash flow	
ROA	= Return on assets	= Net profit + financial expenses/equity+debt
ROCE	= Return on capital employed	= EBIT/equity + interest bearing net debt
ROE	= Return on equity	= Net result / equity
WACC	= Weighted average cost of debt	= Weighted average cost of equity and debt

The profitability of a company using Formula 3 can improve by increasing the operating profit, capital turnover, or both. The operative management of a company, mill, or paper machine can influence profitability with immediate effect as Table 3 indicates.

Cost structure and management accounting

Table 3. Effect of operating profit and capital turnover on profitability.

Effect of operating profit and capital turnover on profitability		
	Operating profit	Capital turnover
Increased product prices	increases	increases
Lower manufacturing costs	increases	-
Increased production without investments	increases	increases
Investments to increase production	increases	decreases
Low investments	decreases	increases
Decrease of working capital by reduction of stocks or current receivables or both	-	increases

One can compare the profitability of a company with that of others by the above two measures – operating profit and capital turnover. The du Pont curve comparison is very informative for company and mill management personnel.

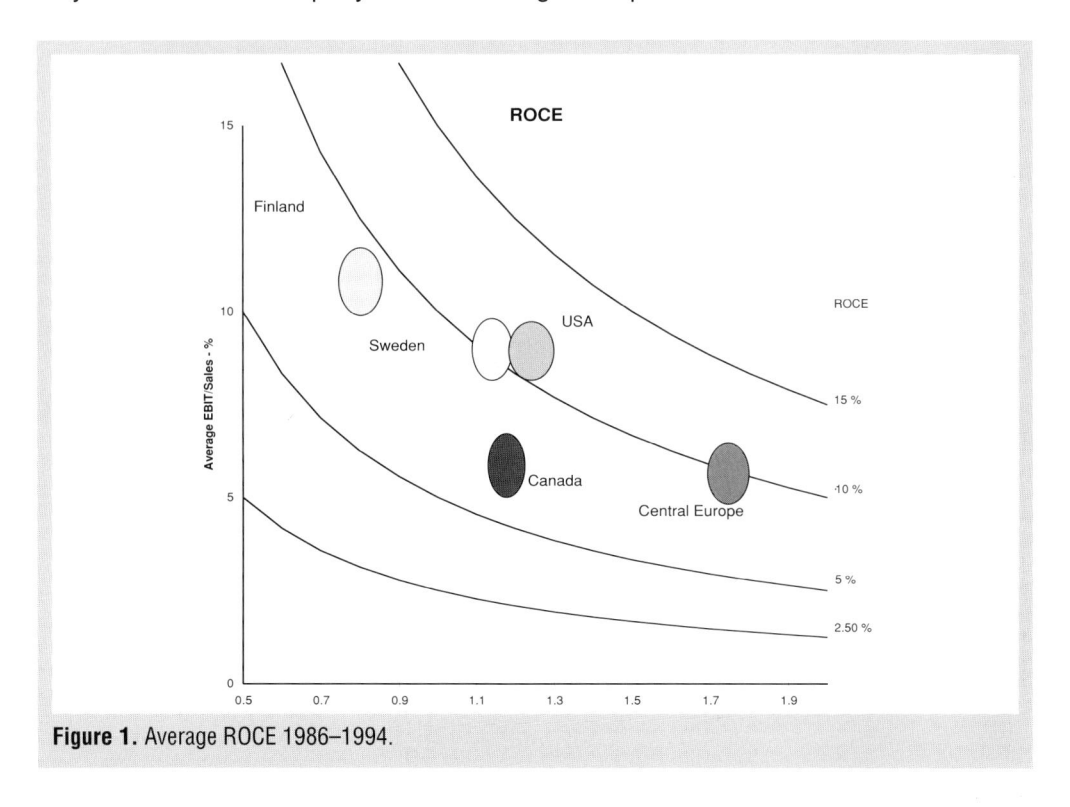

Figure 1. Average ROCE 1986–1994.

CHAPTER 7

Figure 1 compares forest industry companies in certain countries showing the following conclusions:
1. The operating margin in Finland and Sweden has been higher than in the United States and Canada.
2. Capital turnover has been lower in Finland and Sweden than in the United States and Canada.

These two conclusions lead to guidelines for further analysis.
1. The investment rate in Finland and Sweden has been higher than in the United States and Canada. This has led to the situation indicated in Figure 1.
2. It is probable that Scandinavian companies were EBIT or EBITD driven during the 1980s and early 1990s. The objective was to maximize EBIT or EBITD. The best way to do this was through high investment levels. These increased operating margins – both EBITD and EBIT – but lowered capital turnover as the figure shows.

Although different depreciation rules in different countries cause a small margin of error in comparing operating margins of companies, the results and conclusions drawn from Figure 1 are reasonably accurate. As return on capital employed has gained importance due to the concept of shareholder value, many Scandinavian companies have allocated balance sheet responsibility to divisions, mills, or both during the 1990s, rather than having capital allocated at the company level only. This has led to the following changes in division and mill operative management compared with the past:
1. Investment ideas receive more careful analysis since return on capital often decreases especially for large investments.
2. The volume of working capital was formerly of little concern to the division or mill management, since there was no return on capital responsibility. A high volume of working capital meant an easy life. Good service due to high stock levels generated few complaints from customers plus slow activity to reduce receivables – an unpleasant task for the sales force. The reduction of working capital by lowering stocks and receivables is an effective method to release capital for other purposes such as profitable investments or simply to lower capital employed and increase returns through high capital turnover.

3 Shareholder value

3.1 General

The different profitability measures defined in section 7.2 (ROI, ROE, ROCE, etc.) are all widely used and well known methods to measure business performance. However, these methods have certain distinct limitations. They do not set the right target for profitability, nor do they show how capital structure affects results.

Company value increases when the return on invested capital is greater than the cost of capital. Conversely, if the return on invested capital is less than the cost of capital, the company value depreciates, and the value of investment decreases. The primary

Cost structure and management accounting

focus should there be on Economic Value Added (EVA), which is the difference between the interest on capital invested and the cost of capital, multiplied by the capital employed. True value is created when EVA > 0.

3.2 EVA as a concept

EVA is intended to measure the creation of shareholder value, i.e., the effect of a company's result on share prices (=shareholder wealth). EVA is calculated on the basis of capital invested and the required return on it (=cost of capital). This is then compared to operating profit. Capital invested is fixed assets plus net working capital or, in other words, all financing that has demand for returns.

The EVA formula can be defined in several ways:
EVA = actual return on capital − return requirement (cost of capital)
EVA = (EBIT - taxes) − (WACC x capital invested)
EVA = (ROCE after tax − WACC) x capital invested

Section 7.2 defines the above factors with the exception of WACC (Weighted Average Cost of Capital), which is formed of two components. The first is the cost of debt financing, and the second the cost of equity financing.

Cost of debt

The cost of debt is usually based on long term risk free lending rate, i.e., long term government bond interest rate plus risk premium. In the autumn of 1997 risk free interest rates were approximately 6%, and risk premiums approximately 0.5% for high quality companies. The effective cost of debt is calculated by deducting the taxation factor. This means, that the cost is reduced by the tax rate. If the tax rate is 30%, the effective cost of debt is
6.5% - 0.3 x 6.5% = 4.55%.

Cost of equity

Cost of equity is the return that shareholders expect to receive. This can be derived from the equity markets as the return of the average market portfolio. The difference between risk free interest and the return of the average market portfolio is called the risk premium for equity investments. This is normally 5–6%. Risk premium is adjusted to conform to the risk related to a particular share or industry. This adjustment factor (Beta) for the forest industry has been 1.1–1.2, meaning that the adjusted risk factor is 5.5–7.2%. Beta values over 1 mean that the share is more volatile than the market on the average.

Cost of equity for the forest industry, assuming a risk free rate of 6%, is therefore 6% + (5.5–7.2)% = 11.5–13.2%.

CHAPTER 7

3.3 EVA and the market value of a company

Market Value Added (MVA) is the difference between a company's market value (=number of shares x prevailing share price on stock exchange) and its employed capital. MVA therefore reflects the company's success in investing capital in the past and the probable success of its new capital investment in the future. MVA is equal to the present value of future years' EVA, meaning the market's assessment of the company management's ability to allocate capital efficiently and generate returns above its cost of capital.

High MVA reflects the following:
1. The company management feels a responsibility towards their shareholders
2. Investment decisions are expected to give a return in excess of WACC, in other words, EVA is positive.

A high MVA makes it possible for a company to utilize the equity market to finance promising projects or to make new acquisitions or mergers.

Table 4. Influence of shareholder value on company capital costs.

	Company A	Company B
Profit 1995	100	100
Number of shares	50	50
Earning per share (EPS)	2	2
Price earning ratio (P/E)	10	5
Share price	20	10
Dividend per share 30% of profit 1995	0.6	0.6
New equity 20 shares at current share price	40	20

Table 4 illustrates how the same number of shares generates twice the amount of equity capital for company A, with a high MVA, compared to company B with low MVA. In the case of a merger between companies A and B, creating a new company AB, the equity of AB is divided 66% to company A shareholders and 34% to company B shareholders. The fact that capital employed, profits, EPS, etc. have been identical for companies A and B, does not affect the above ratio.

3.4 Value based management

Value can be created only if the management of a company invests capital at returns that exceed the cost of capital. Value Based Management (VBM) focuses on the decision making process at all levels of the organization, facilitating the maximization of its value. VBM requires two essential elements:
1. The senior management must have a solid understanding of the variables that drive the value of a company.
2. Usually an organization cannot act directly on values but has to act on issues it can influence, for example customer satisfaction, capital expenditure, costs, etc. The identification of these issues forms an important part of VBM.

Cost structure and management accounting

Any improvement in the company value derives from one of three sources:
1. Growth
2. Improved profitability
3. Increased free cash flow.

Table 5 gives an example of the value drivers that should be specified for each individual business unit. Conceptually these drivers are also dealt with in section 7.9.

Table 5. Value drivers for individual business units.

		VALUE DRIVERS	
	High level financial driver	Operational drivers	
Value	Profitability	Increase price margin	Rising sales prices	Developing products and brands
		More sales from same assets	Reducing costs	Recognizing profitable customers Enhancing efficiency Cutting overheads
	Free cash flow	Reduce working capital	Cutting working capital	Sourcing activities Seeking low cost materials
		Asset sales	Selling non-performing assets	Cutting inventories Shortening credit periods
	Growth	Investment in profitable business	Investments	Lengthening periods of accounts payables Capital expenditure Acquisitions
			Restructuring businesses	Capturing marketing channels

4 Investment behavior in certain countries

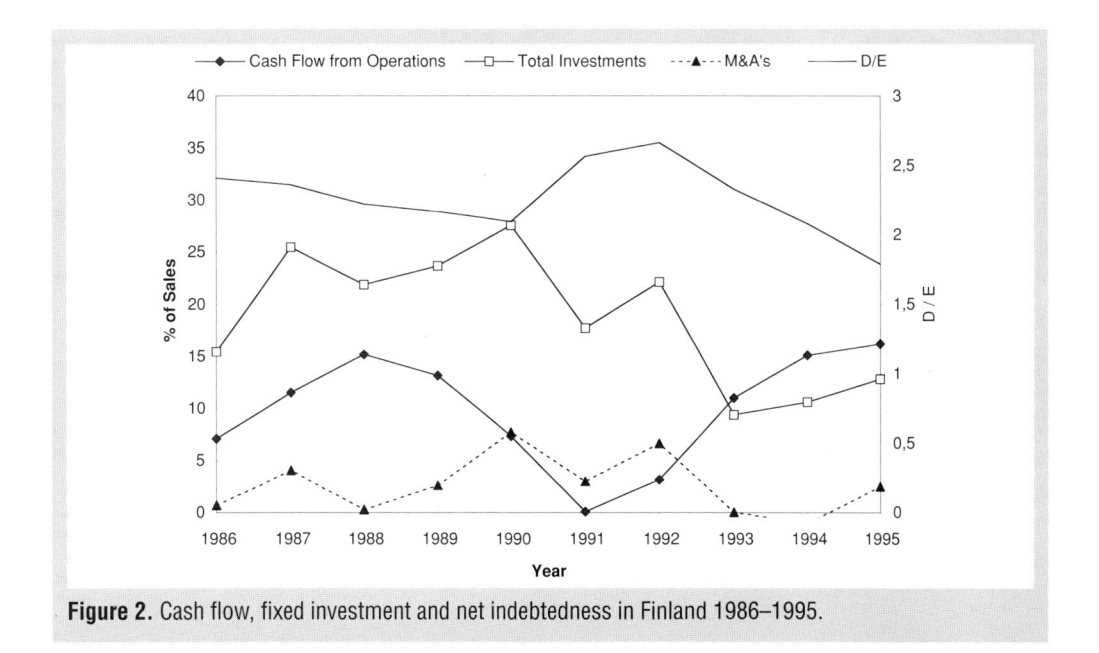

Figure 2. Cash flow, fixed investment and net indebtedness in Finland 1986–1995.

CHAPTER 7

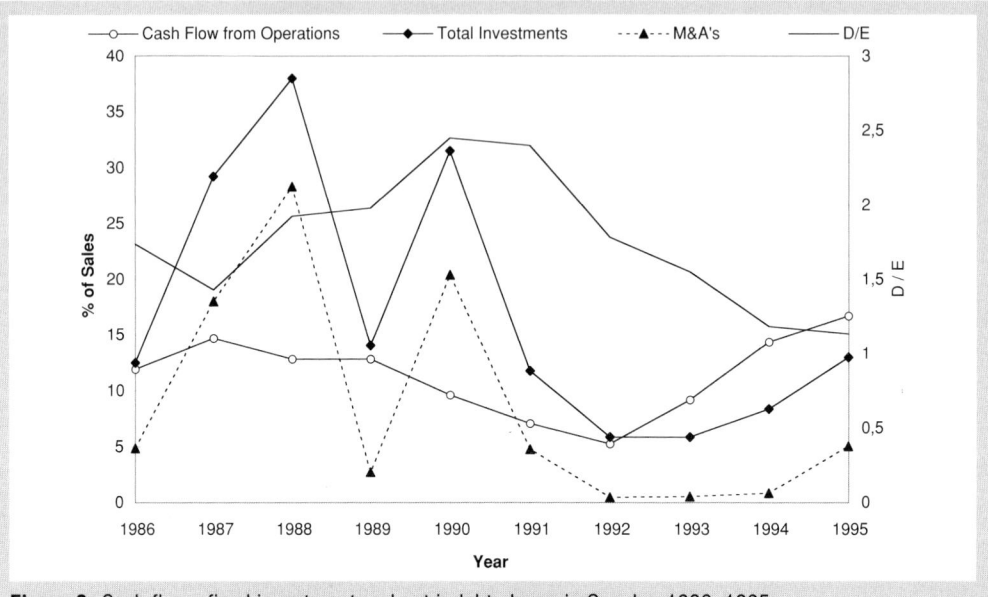

Figure 3. Cash flow, fixed investment and net indebtedness in Sweden 1986–1995.

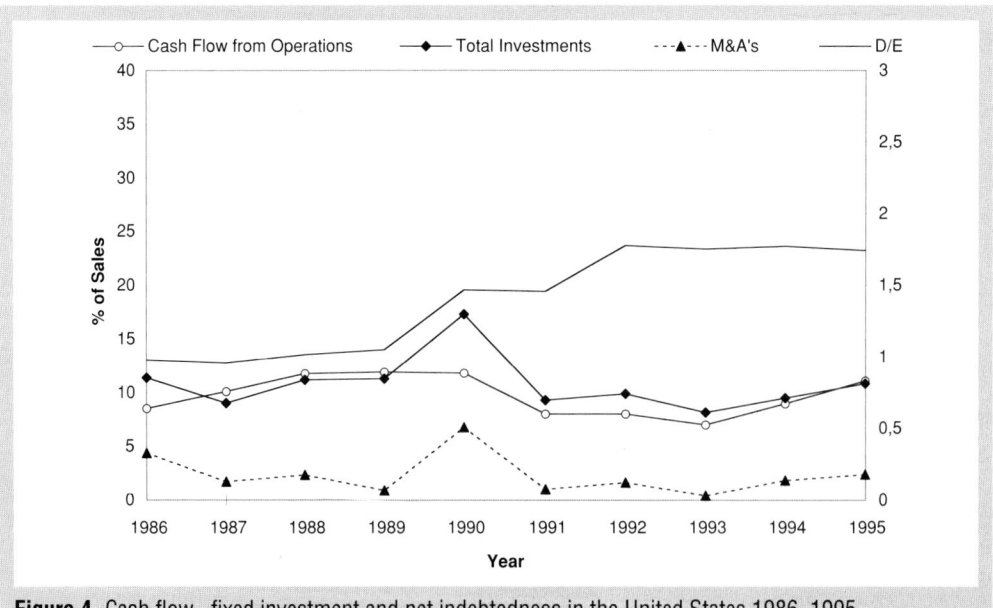

Figure 4. Cash flow, fixed investment and net indebtedness in the United States 1986–1995.

Figure 5. Cash flow, fixed investment and net indebtedness in Canada 1986 – 1995.

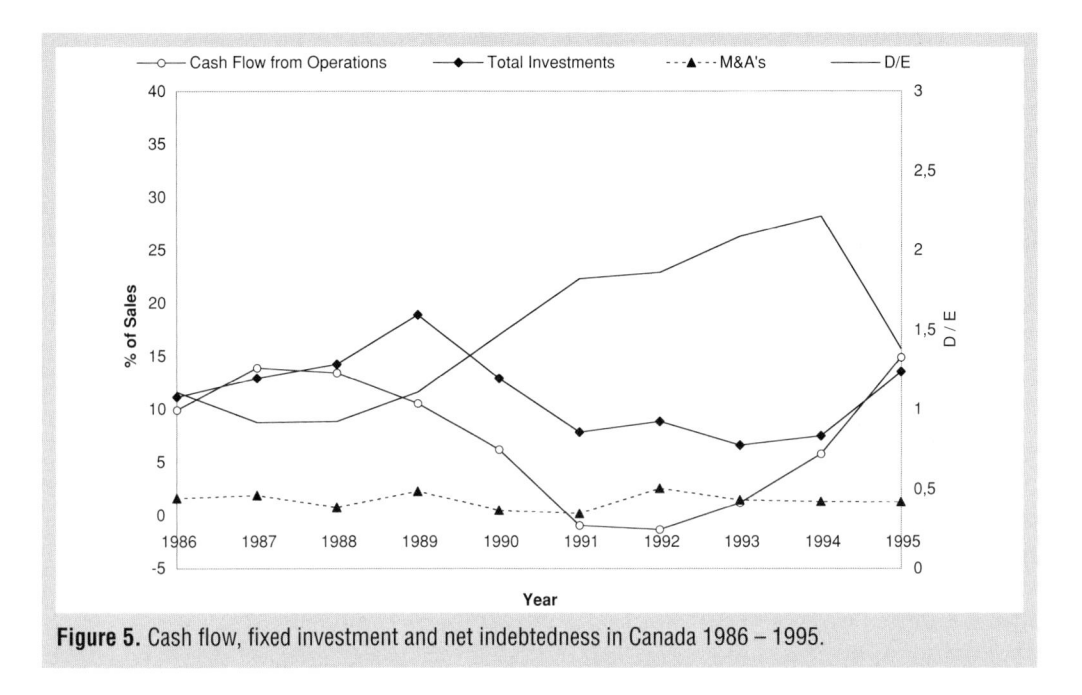

Figures 2–5 show the cash flow, fixed investments and net indebtedness development for 1986–1995 in Finland, Sweden, Canada and the United States using the companies in Table 14 in Chapter 6. The following conclusions result:

1. Scandinavian companies especially in Finland have invested more than their cash flow during 1986–1993. This has increased their indebtedness to a high level. During 1991–1995, this trend reversed, and net indebtedness has started to decline.
2. U.S. companies have investments approximately equal to their cash flow.
3. Canadian companies have clearly also invested more than the cash flow generated causing their burden of debt to grow until 1994.

It is therefore possible to conclude that at least for the Finnish forest industry, profitability has been too low for the selected investment level considering the increase of indebtedness. If the Finnish industry had wanted to maintain investments with the actual cash flow without incurring more debts, the only remaining solutions would have been the sale of properties or an increase of its own equity. Both methods were widely use at the end of the 1980s. This explains the slow increase of the debt to equity ratio.

5 Appropriate investment levels

One fundamental question occurs. What is the appropriate investment level of a forest company in the long term? Using research in the 1980s in Finland[1], the average figure should be approximately 9% per year. This figure includes both replacement investments and development investments necessary to maintain the earning capability and market share of the company. Using this figure as a starting point, the gross margin or EBITD level of a forest company can be roughly calculated as Table 6 indicates.

CHAPTER 7

Table 6. Gross margin requirement or EBITD for a forest company.

Investments	9 % of sales
Net interest costs, depending on capital structure	2-8 % of sales
Dividends	approx. 1 % of sales
Taxes	approx. 1 % of sales
Total EBITD requirement	**13-19 % of sales**

Table 6 assumes that the change in working capital is negligible.

It can be argued that the investment figure of 9% does not sufficiently consider the expansion necessary to increase the market share. Assuming that the figures in Table 6 are sufficient to increase production volumes by 3% per year in the long term, a 4–5% per year increase in production volumes would require 3 additional percentage units per year with the added assumption that capital turnover for a new mill or machine is 0.5, as indicated earlier in this book. This would correspondingly increase the EBITD requirements from 13–19% to 16–22% in the above example.

As Table 15 in Chapter 6 shows, Finland is the only country to achieve these EBITD figures assuming a depreciation level of 6%.

6 Management accounting

The purpose of management accounting is to provide the company and mill management with follow-up information of the company's financial performance. In addition it provides in advance information that helps to choose the best and most profitable alternatives and plans in a given situation.

The following two main factors determine the quality level of the management accounting system in a mill:
1. Delivery time of the information required by the mill management.
2. Reliability of the information provided.
   Many situations require information and answers from a mill's management accounting system. It is a difficult task to construct a system that will provide correct answers to a wide variety of questions quickly and easily. Sometimes ambitious attempts to develop complete systems have resulted in such complex models that the operative management cannot judge the accuracy of the results.

Often the mill management requires answers from the management accounting system to the following questions:
1. Which paper machine in a mill with many such paper machines should manufacture a certain order to maximize profits?
2. At what sales price level should a paper machine be shut down, rather than accept orders for manufacture?

Cost structure and management accounting

3. At what sales price does the paper machine and mill achieve an acceptable ROI level?
4. Is the calculated profit increase for a contemplated investment sufficiently large to justify its implementation?
5. Is implementation of a planned change in the working practices on a paper machine worthwhile and profitable?

A mill's management accounting system is often built to provide answers to questions 1, 2 and 3. Calculating the results for different action plans for these questions has proved to be useful, as comparisons between different solutions sometimes reveal avenues of action not immediately obvious.

The integration of mills such as pulp with paper mill, saw mill with pulp mill, etc., increases the complexity of management accounting systems. Each production unit often has its own system. Although these systems give correct answers and information for the unit they cover, the answers may be incorrect for the whole integrate.

Consider an example to provide clarification. A paper mill with one paper machine undergoes integration with an adjacent pulp mill and uses it as its sole source of raw material. Both the paper mill and the pulp mill have their own management accounting systems, and each forms a separate profit unit. An agreement specifies that the paper mill will buy the pulp at market cost adjusted by drying costs.

Paper prices begin to decline due to over capacity, and the paper mill reaches a situation where sales prices fall below the variable costs of the paper mill. Accordingly the paper mill management decides to shut down the paper machine and wait for better-priced orders to arrive. Then the pulp mill must also stop, since its main customer has stopped needing pulp. This is unfortunate for the pulp mill, because the sales price paid by the paper mill would have covered all their variable costs and some fixed costs.

In this situation it is evident that the decision is incorrect, because the losses acquired will be larger with both mills shut down. Before making the decision to shut down the entire integrate – question 2 above, a separate calculation should have considered the entire operation.

The above situation is less likely to occur where the pulp and paper mill management communicates daily even if they do form separate profit units. If the paper mill uses pulp produced by a pulp mill located in another country, the above situation is more likely to arise despite the fact that the same company owns the paper and pulp mills.

Costs usually fall into the following categories:
1. Variable costs (= production related costs)
2. Fixed costs
3. Capital costs.

CHAPTER 7

Variable costs depend entirely on production volumes. When production stops, these costs are zero. Typical items are raw materials, chemicals, additives, etc. Energy costs such as heat and electricity are often production related costs. This is not always correct, since heat and energy costs include a portion of fixed costs. In situations where the heat and energy consumption varies widely from a predetermined level used as a basis for cost calculation, it is particularly prone to inaccuracy.

Production volumes have no influence on fixed costs. Typical cost items are operating and maintenance personnel costs directly related to the profit unit and spare parts such as wires and felts.

General costs usually form a group not directly attributable to a certain production unit or paper machine. Typical general costs are mill management, administration, safety, environment etc. Division or company overheads allocated to a specific mill can also form part of this cost group.

Capital costs allocated to a mill are time related. Some mills include only interest costs, while others include both interest and depreciation.

As a general rule, only the costs that a profit unit can influence should be used and allocated to the management accounting system of a profit unit. In this way, the system reflects reality since they are costs and matters that a profit unit can handle or change if necessary. This rule does limit the scope of the management accounting system as noted earlier in this chapter.

Another rule of thumb when considering the reliability of the management accounting system is to use it for operative matters where the changes contemplated or alternatives compared are close to one another. More drastic measures for analysis such as shutting down a paper machine or mill require greater caution when analyzing the results given by the management accounting system.

An example of the difficulties experienced in considering the correct input values in a mill's management accounting system is the correct energy cost for heat and electricity. The electricity unit costs contain a fixed amount per year that is often divided per anticipated annual consumption to make it a variable component. This method is often practical and meaningful, since the fixed part is often relatively small compared with the variable part. Allocation based on consumption is therefore easier. For heat or steam, a similar situation arises, since the heat generation unit – a steam or recovery boiler – has certain fixed capital and personnel costs that can be divided by anticipated total annual heat consumption. This makes the fixed portion of these costs variable with easier allocation to the user.

In addition to the above difficulties concerning unit costs, there is the problem of consumption. For instance, the electricity consumption of a groundwood or TMP plant is production related – a variable cost. On a paper machine, the electricity consumption is more time than production related. The paper machine consumes approximately the same amount of electricity while the unit is running with or without the production of paper.

Cost structure and management accounting

Table 7 shows the cost structure of a pulp mill, and Table 8 presents that of a newsprint mill.

Table 7. Cost structure of a 500 000 tons/year softwood chemical pulp mill at full production.

1. Production related costs / variable costs	
Wood	31.0
Chemicals	7.9
Energy	0.7
Operating materials & services	10.7
Total variable costs	**50.3**
2. Time related / fixed costs	
Maintenance materials	5.2
Personnel and administration	3.3
Others	5
Total fixed costs	**13.5**
3. Capital costs	**36.2**
4. Total	**100.0**

Table 8. Cost structure of a 450 000 tons/year newsprint mill with two modern paper machines at full production.

1. Production related costs / variable costs	
Raw material (wood, waste paper)	23.8
Chemicals	6.7
Packing materials	2.0
Energy	13.2
Operating materials	3.6
Total variable costs	**49.3**
2. Time related / fixed costs	
Maintenance materials	5.5
Personnel and administration	13.7
Others	4.3
Total fixed costs	**23.5**
3. Capital costs	**27.2**
4. Total	**100.0**

7 Comparison of order profitability

Comparison of the profitability of different orders on a given paper machine is an important task for the paper machine, mill superintendent, and the sales force. All these

CHAPTER 7

people must know the profitability ranking of customers and orders to select the best orders when order inflow is good. Long term efforts can and should also be directed toward customers whose orders give the highest profitability to increase the volume of their orders further. It is equally important to eliminate or to lower the order inflow from those customers whose orders give the lowest returns. All these factors have a great impact on shareholder value (7.3) and are important elements of value based management. Table 9 shows an example of a profitability calculation for an order.

Table 9. Profitability calculation for a given order based on Table 8.

1. Sales income	(currency unit/t)	105
2. Variable costs	(currency unit/t)	49.3
3. Contribution margin	(currency unit/t)	55.7
4. (contribution margin x rate of production) currency unit / t x t / h = 55.7 x 450000/8400 = 55.7 x currency unit / h = 2984 currency unit/ h			

The orders that give the highest contribution per hour are the most profitable to produce. It should be noted that the selection criterion is contribution per hour not contribution per ton.

If the contribution margin falls below zero, it is better to stop production. This assumes that all fixed costs such as labor are time related – the production volume has no impact on them. In practice, this was the situation in most European mills in the mid 1990s. Although better than a zero margin, a low contribution margin means heavy losses because it is not possible to cover fixed costs and the capital costs.

For an order to be profitable, the contribution per hour it generates should cover all fixed and capital costs per hour.

In cases where the paper mill has more than one paper machine that can produce a certain order, the selection of the paper machine becomes more complicated. The main rule is to maximize the mill's total contribution per hour rather than that of a single paper machine. The example in Table 10 illustrates this situation.

Table 10. Example of cost calculation for a paper mill with two paper machines.

	PM1	PM2	Total
Contribution per hour	100	130	230
If the order is split and produced on both PM's, the mill contribution per hour is 230 as illustrated above. If the order is produced on PM2 only, and at the same time PM1 can run an order with 100 or higher contribution per hour, this is the right decision. If, however, the question asked by management is on which PM the order should be produced to get the highest margin, the following situation may occur:			
Contribution per hour	50	130	180

This example illustrates the importance of asking the right questions.

In a mill with many paper machines, one can calculate the optimum production program by comparing alternative production programs for the whole mill and selecting the optimum from these.

Cost structure and management accounting

The size of the working capital requirement and its impact on interest costs for a certain order or production program often does not receive consideration due to the difficulty of correct allocation. Interest on working capital is often considered as a fixed cost for a production unit and evenly distributed to all orders. With modern management accounting systems, it is possible to allocate the exact working capital requirement to each order considering storage time of finished and semifinished products – particularly important for sheeted products, where payment times can vary 10–150 days, etc. The impact can be surprisingly large.

8 Factors affecting production rate

The production rate on a paper machine naturally has a strong effect on production costs and therefore on profitability. The production rate in tons/h depends on two factors.
1. Momentary production
   Width, speed, and substance of production determine momentary production. Figure 6 shows the calculation for the relation between speed and substance for a given paper machine.

The following general rules apply:
- The paper machine drive or the wet end of the machine limits production when producing low substances.
- The drying capacity limits production rate of high substances.

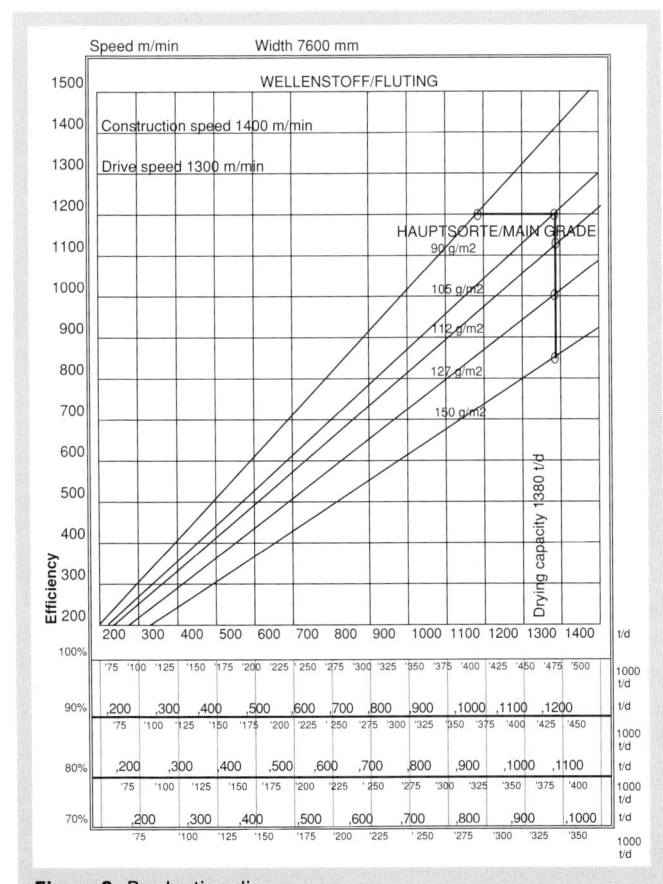

Figure 6. Production diagram.

Sometimes the runability limits production particularly for low substances. This means that the paper machine must run slower than the drive or wet end capacity would allow to avoid frequent breaks or certain specific quality problems.

CHAPTER 7

If the wet end limits the maximum speed, the paper machine is wet-end limited. Typical reasons for wet-end limits are the following:
- The wire section is too short and cannot remove sufficient water at high speeds.
- The capacity of the pumps, cleaners, or both before the headbox is too low.
- The headbox flows increase to levels that the headbox cannot handle with acceptable formation of paper and stable cross machine profiles.

If the drying section limits the speed of the paper machine, the paper machine is dry-end limited. This applies to many board machines.

2. Efficiency of production

Efficiency of production is an important technical parameter on any given paper machine. It efficiently illustrates the technical success of operations on a paper machine during a given period and allows making continuous comparisons over a long period. It is also a useful tool when comparing the performance of two different paper machines provided they are producing the same grade. Efficiency comparisons are common for machines making newsprint, SC paper, and LWC paper. Efficiency comparisons for machines producing woodfree papers are more uncertain, since the amount of reels vs. sheets, the substance range, and other similar factors adversely affect the accuracy of such comparisons.

The following equation provides a definition of efficiency of production:

$$P_n = \eta \times P_m \tag{9}$$

where P_n is saleable production (also called net production)
P_m is momentary production
η is total efficiency

Total efficiency has the following components:

η^1 is operating efficiency. This represents the time the paper machine is not running due to felt and wire changes, maintenance work, etc. For a newsprint or SC paper machine, η^1 is approximately 94% – annual average.

η^2 is machine efficiency. This represents the time used for breaks, grade changes, etc. For a newsprint or SC paper machine, η^2 is approximately 95% – annual average.

η^3 is trim efficiency. This represents the width after winder – the width sold to customers – compared with the maximum width at the paper machine reeler. On a newsprint or SC paper machine, η^3 is usually 99% – annual average.

η^4 is finishing efficiency. This represents the loss between paper machine reeler and saleable production. On a newsprint or SC paper machine, η^4 is usually 95% – annual average.

Total efficiency is the product of all these individual efficiencies as Formula 10 shows.

$$\eta = \eta^1 \times \eta^2 \times \eta^3 \times \eta^4 \tag{10}$$

According to the above figures for a newsprint or SC paper machine, the total efficiency would be

η = 0.94 x 0.95 x 0.99 x 0.95 = 0.84

This means an 84% annual average.

The following factors should be taken into account when comparing the efficiency figures of paper machines in different countries:
1. Time span considered
   Efficiency figures are calculated on a daily, monthly, or annual basis. Longer periods give lower figures.
2. The basis of momentary production can be the actual momentary production or the maximum achievable momentary production. The latter can lower the efficiency figures calculated, since it adds an additional efficiency component of speed.
3. Some mills run 365 days per year, and others run 330–350 days annually due to summer holidays, statutory holidays, etc. Maintenance often occurs during such shut downs. This improves the operating efficiency compared to those mills running 365 days per year.
4. Uniformity of production – order size, length of production runs, reels vs. sheets, etc. – between different paper machines is difficult to define and compare. It does have a strong impact on efficiency.

The operative mill and paper machine management should continuously monitor the development of efficiency and its components. Management should set targets and implement programs to improve efficiency.

Paper mill and paper machine management personnel often have the task of maintaining profitability with minimal price increases despite increased costs. The answer to this problem is a higher production rate through higher momentary production or with higher efficiency. In practice, both usually occur.

CHAPTER 7

Table 11. Annual production increase necessary to offset 3% increase in variable costs and 4% increase in fixed costs, assuming a 2% price increase of sales.

Base year			
	1. Income	105	currency/t
	2. Variable costs	49.3	currency/t
	3. Fixed costs	50.7	currency/t
	4. Profit during base year	5	currency/t
Base year + 1			
	1. Income	V x 1.02 x 105	= Vx 107.10
	2. Variable costs	V x 1.03 x 49.3	= V x 50.78
	3. Fixed costs	1.04 x 50.7	= 52.73
	4. Profit during year 1		= 5
	(V x 107.10 - V x 50.78) - 52.73 = 5		V = 1.0250
	VOLUME MUST ACCORDINGLY BE INCREASED BY 2.5 % i.e. 11 250 tons		

Table 11 illustrates the calculations based on the cost structure given in Table 8

9 Evaluation of development investment

To improve the profitability of a paper machine, the mill and machine management must consider a variety of alternative measures to implement to increase revenues or reduce costs. Management accounting can determine the best alternative. Since management accounting primarily provides solutions related to production planning such as profitability comparison of different orders, care is necessary not to make mistakes caused by applying this method in a general way. Energy costs can be a particular stumbling block.

The following example illustrates the situation.

A paper machine is dry-end limited because of a poor press section. Its steam section is also old and worn. The unit therefore has high specific steam consumption per ton of output. The paper machine superintendent proposes a modernization of the press section and replacement of the steam system at the drying part.

The plan is to achieve the following benefits:
1. Higher speed
2. Lower steam consumption due to higher dryness after the press section and lower specific steam consumption at the drying portion.

By using the standard unit costs for steam, it can be proved that the pay back of the investment would be approximately four years, not considering higher speed or volume.

Cost structure and management accounting

The standard unit costs for steam usually consist of both variable and fixed costs. The fixed costs including personnel, maintenance, and capital costs for steam generation can be significant and must be paid regardless of steam consumption. If the share of fixed costs of the total steam costs is 50%, the pay back time in the above example doubles from four to eight years.

The above example gains more weight if the paper mill is integrated to a pulp mill, and steam is supplied by the pulp mill energy block. A modern pulp mill generates more steam than it can use. All or some of the steam costs paid by the paper mill to the pulp mill are zero from the integrate's viewpoint. If the pulp and paper mill have separate management accounting systems, this is not always evident.

Finally the above example shows that lower steam consumption by the paper mill means less electricity production from the back-pressure turbine. This further lengthens the pay back time.

The final conclusion drawn from the above example may possibly be that the lower steam consumption does not reduce costs sufficiently to justify the investment, although the standard unit cost calculation according to management accounting seems to justify the investment. In such a case, only the higher production volume achieved through higher running speed could then justify the investment.

The pay back time – additional, new revenues or cost savings divided by investment – for marginal investments should by rule of thumb be less than 3–4 years to consider the investment seriously. The reason is that the higher output in many cases cannot be achieved due to limitations and new complications and bottlenecks that the implemented investment reveals elsewhere in the production line.

Table 12 gives some rough guidelines for small and medium size investments.

Table 12. Profitability criteria for marginal investments.

	Payback time (years)	Implementation
1	< 1	Safe and good investment, which should be implemented as soon as possible
2	1-2	Good investment, which should be implemented during next suitable shut-down (e.g. Christmas or other statutory holiday)
3	2-4	Requires very careful analysis before implementation
4	> 4	Usually a questionable proposal

CHAPTER 7

10 Distribution of economic information to the operating floor

Distribution of relevant economic information to the operating crew improves working motivation, production, and quality level. The positive impact can increase further with training and education about economic facts provided by the paper mill management. Suitable examples are the following:

1. How large are the financial losses caused by an unexpected shut down lasting one hour?
2. How much extra revenue results from lowering waste due to bad quality by one percentage unit?
3. How much extra revenue comes from increasing paper machine speed by 10 m/min?
4. How many complaints relate to the paper machine, and what are their consequent costs?
5. What cost reduction will be achieved by increasing the filler content in the furnish by one percentage unit?

The above questions are only limited samples. The mill and machine management should select the subjects using careful analysis of the most common and important questions a specific production line encounters in daily operation. Being taught simple, clear solutions to the problems they are likely to face, the operating crew has the knowledge and ability to act in a well founded manner to achieve the optimum result on their specific paper machine or pulp mill.

Sources

1 Finnish Forest Industry Federation

CHAPTER 8

Investment decision

1	**Preparation of major capital expenditure decisions**	**127**
1.1	General	127
1.2	Pre-feasibility studies	127
1.3	Basic engineering and feasibility	128
1.4	Investment decision	128
1.5	Detailed planning	129
2	**Criteria for profitability and competitiveness**	**129**
2.1	Profitability	129
2.2	Wood paying capacity	133
2.3	Cost competitiveness	133
3	**Ability to take risks**	**136**
4	**Selection criteria for new equipment**	**138**

Investment decision

1 Preparation of major capital expenditure decisions

1.1 General

The forest industry is capital intensive in character, and the lifespan of mills and machines is several decades. Lack of flexibility in the production of a certain paper machine or pulp mill is also a typical characteristic. A major new investment is therefore an irreversible step. The size of the investment also restricts moves in other directions, usually for many years. For these reasons, any large investment decision requires meticulous preparation. Adequate resources are necessary for the preparatory phase, since the costs of this phase are small compared with the total; usually 1–2%. The preparatory work should also make it easier to identify and minimize potential risks.

1.2 Pre-feasibility studies

An early feasibility study is the first step of the preparatory phase. Its purpose is to analyze and determine the general feasibility and success potential of a project. The main elements are the following:

1. Market study:
   The aim of a market study is to estimate future demand and price development. A historical overview of these two factors usually forms the starting point for the analysis. An attempt to estimate the future supply can use either of the two following methods:
   - A supply estimate based on known investment decisions and probable projects, expected shutdowns of existing mills and paper machines, and estimated total capacity increase through minor investments and improvements. The last category is often ignored, but it can increase capacity 1–2% per year. Such a supply estimate is reasonably accurate for periods of 2–3 years. This is a short time considering that the construction time of a new paper machine is 18–20 months from the investment decision.
   - A more difficult and demanding method is analysis of the past behavior of major suppliers, their profitability, expressed objectives and strategies, status of existing mills and machinery, raw material availability, etc. This technique analyzes and defines the general supply outlook and gives information to estimate the medium and long term future supply. Although it is less explicit and quantified, this analysis usually gives valuable information.

CHAPTER 8

The market study also estimates the future development of the quality level. This is especially important for grades using new manufacturing technology or where end users use technologies causing new quality requirements.

2. Raw material availability:

   The availability, quality, and price of raw material are important considerations for any new project. These aspects must therefore be reliably verified. Availability consists of two elements:
   - verification that the required volume of raw material such as wood, recycled fiber, or both does exist
   - verification that the necessary infrastructure and supply organization exists and can supply the required raw material.

3. Preliminary cost competitiveness and profitability analysis:

   To assess these aspects, a general mill design including basic dimensioning for the primary machinery is necessary. This provides information for the preliminary investment budget and manufacturing cost estimate. A preliminary idea of the profitability of the project results from comparing estimated manufacturing costs with estimated sales revenues.

   At this stage, suppliers receive no inquiries for machinery needs, since the mill design is preliminary and general.

1.3 Basic engineering and feasibility

This next phase occurs after the previous if the feasibility study shows the project is viable. It is the basic engineering phase and includes a more detailed mill design, dimensioning, and applications for the necessary permits. The accuracy level of this phase is sufficiently detailed to make inquiries containing specifications for main machinery to potential suppliers. Using the reviewed mill design and the quotations received from suppliers, the feasibility study then includes the reviewed investment cost, construction schedule, profitability and cost competitiveness, and financing plans.

To ensure reliability and satisfactory performance, the basic engineering phase must be sufficiently reliable that the investment and initial budget should be accurate within 1–3% depending on the size and scope of the project. The time required for basic engineering of a paper mill project is normally 4–8 months. In some countries, this phase can take 12–18 months due to application procedures for permits.

1.4 Investment decision

The investment decision can be taken on completion of the basic engineering phase and proof and acceptance of the feasibility of the project. The first step is ordering the main machinery that has a long delivery time. In a paper mill project, this will be the paper machine. In a pulp mill project, the digesters, recovery boiler, or both will be the items. Purchasing requires substantial outlay of capital. Stopping the project after this point is very expensive.

1.5 Detailed planning

Detailed planning starts when the main machinery has been ordered.. This includes all the activities necessary to transform the plans into reality. For this reason, detailed planning is not part of the preparatory phase but is in the execution phase.

Having basic engineering at a level sufficient to allow ordering the main machinery is an important advantage. Detailed planning can then begin immediately after making the investment decision.

2 Criteria for profitability and competitiveness

2.1 Profitability

The most important factor in assessing the feasibility of a project is its profitability in terms of return on investment. The following equation shows the relationship of these items.

$$\text{Return on capital} = \frac{\text{Result}}{\text{Capital employed}} \qquad (1)$$

The return on investment is estimated before making an investment decision. The key problem is that capital must be employed immediately after making the investment decision. This is usually 1–24 months months after the decision. The results only begin to materialize much later.

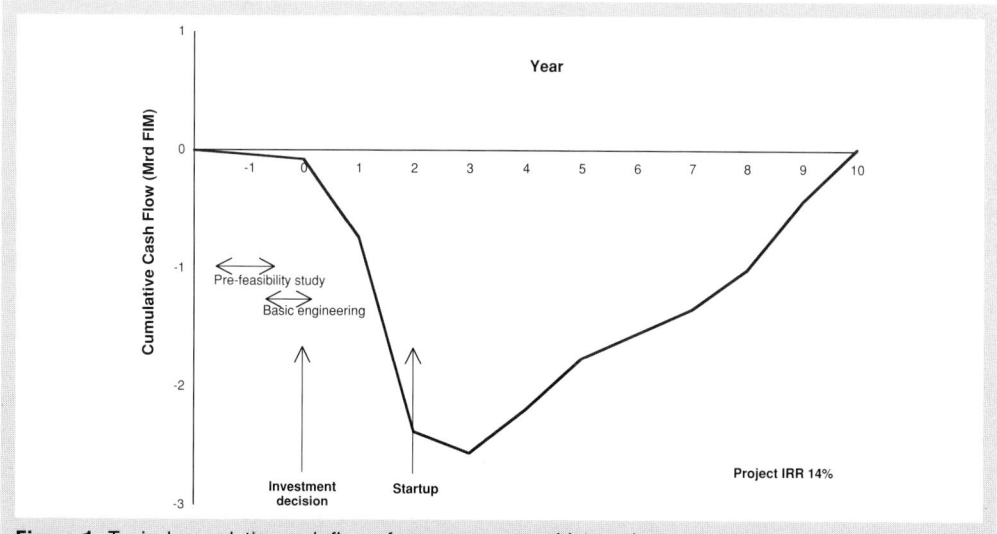

Figure 1. Typical cumulative cash flow of a new paper machine project.

CHAPTER 8

Figure 1 illustrates the cumulative cash flow for a typical paper machine project. One can resolve the difficulty of timing regarding outflow and inflow of money in profitability calculations by calculating the internal rate of return (IRR) of the annual cash flows for a given number of years. The definition of IRR is as follows:

IRR (%)	= the discount rate that equates the present value of the future stream of payments to the initial investment
Stream of payment	= annual cash flows
Initial investment	= total investment at time of investment decision

The advantage of IRR profitability is that it illustrates return expectation with a single figure so that projects having different cash flows during the time of the project are easily comparable by using this method.

In principle, the IRR of a project should be sufficiently high to cover both interest on capital employed and any risk factor. Both factors vary from country to country and from one period to another. One may apply the very rough guidelines of Table 1.

Table 1. Minimum IRR requirement in forest industry projects.

	Min/IRR requirement
1. Large new paper machine or pulp mill project	> 13 %
2. Large modernization project	> 18 %
3. Small modernization project	> 25 %

Modernization projects require a higher IRR figure, since the risk factors are higher due to some machinery remaining in its old form. Any improved performance such as higher speed of the old parts is not always certain, since predictive tests are not always possible before modernization. Unexpected new complications may also arise after a modernization project. The higher IRR requirement should cover this type of risk factor.

Investment decision

Sensitivity of profitability

Figure 2. Sensitivity of IRR.

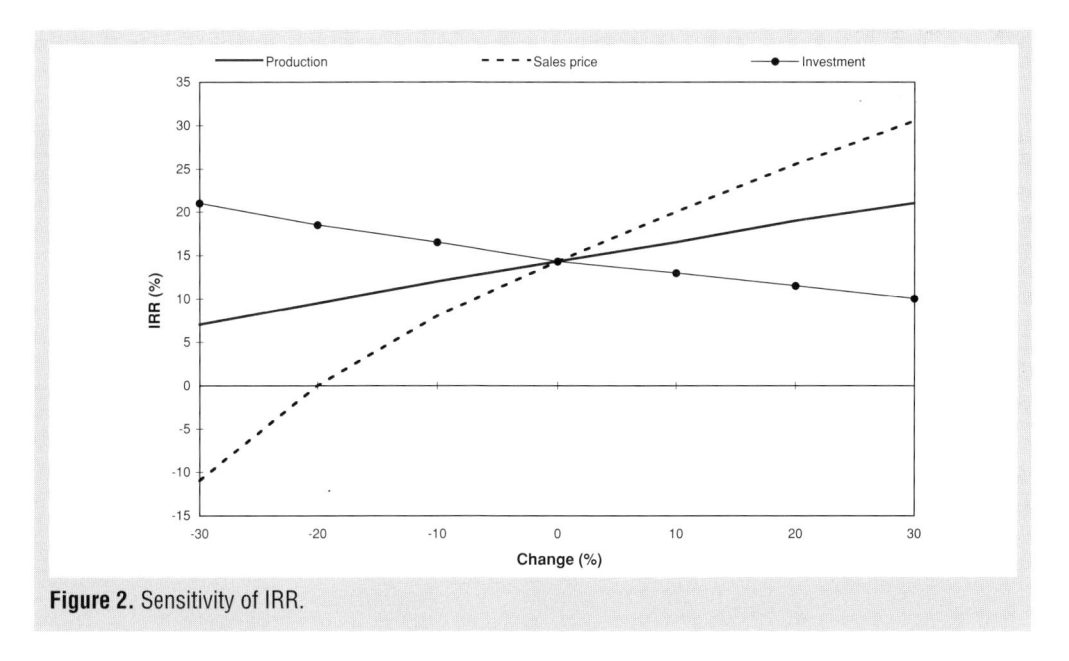

Figure 2 illustrates the sensitivity of a typical paper machine project and leads to the following conclusions:
1. The most sensitive factor is the sales price. Extreme care should therefore be used in analyzing this aspect. Unfortunately, unexpected market developments and cyclical factors usually make sales price forecasts unreliable.
2. The least sensitive factor is the investment cost. This means that one should not make investment cost savings that endanger the production or sales price. On the other hand, the company itself has almost total control over the investment cost. With careful basic engineering, no unexpected increases or decreases in investment cost should occur. The nature of this factor is therefore diametrically opposed to that of the sales price in terms of reliability.

Impact of cycles on profitability

Most forest industry products are cyclical in demand and prices. As a result, project timing – start up time in the price cycle – has a great impact on profitability in general and cash flows during the first operational years in particular, as Figure 3 demonstrates.

CHAPTER 8

Figure 3. Profitability of a large forest industry project showing IRR percentage.

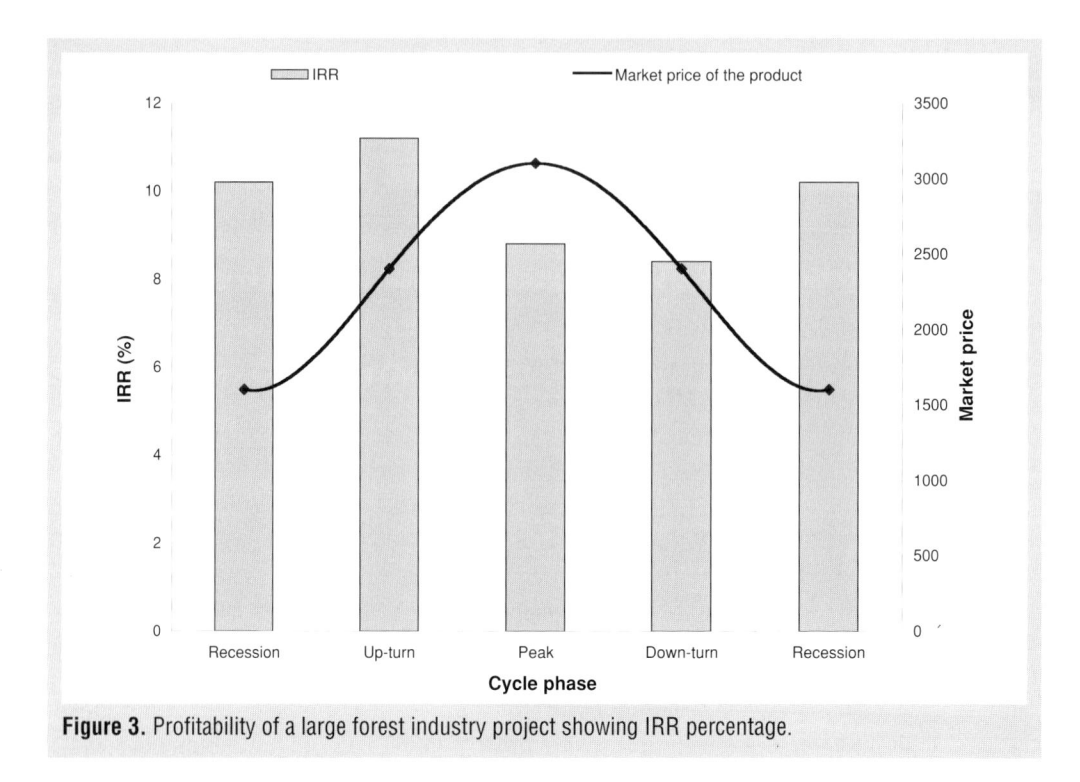

Figure 3 illustrates the following facts:
1. The best start-up time in the cycle is during recession and up turn. Almost full production volume is achieved 2–3 years after startup when prices are increasing and the peak of the cycle is approaching. The project then enjoys maximum product prices and volumes. Revenues at this point are close to the critical point of the project.
2. The worst start-up time is during a peak or down turn. Although prices are high, the production volume during the first and possibly second year of operation has not achieved full level. Sales revenues and profits therefore suffer. When production finally achieves its full volume 2–3 years after startup, product prices and profits are down.
3. The difference between optimum start-up time in the cycle vs. the worst case is three percentage units measured with IRR. This is significant.

One can demonstrate that the cash flow generated by a large new forest industry project with optimum vs. worst case start-up timing during the first three operational years alone can differ by FIM 800–1 000 million (approx. USD 200 million) for a FIM 2 500 million (approx. USD 550 million) investment, with sales estimated to be FIM 2 000 million at full production. This difference is huge, and in the worst case scenario, it requires additional financing arrangements in most cases.

2.2 Wood paying capacity

When a scarcity of wood exists, calculating the wood paying capacity (WPC) of a project is useful in addition to profitability measured by IRR. The following equation provides the definition using FIM as a sample currency:

$$\text{WPC} = \frac{M - (V + P - R)}{W} \text{FIM/m}^3 \qquad (2)$$

where M is Sales income, FIM
V Manufacturing costs, FIM
P Capital costs, FIM
R Wood costs, FIM
W Wood consumption, m^3.

In general WPC increases with higher value-added products unless the return on capital factor, P, is very high.

Calculation of WPC and profitability requires knowing the sales price. As indicated earlier, this is an uncertain factor. Cyclical variations and long term price developments are difficult to predict with reasonable accuracy and reliability. In addition, different forest products follow different patterns. In product comparisons, the product's cyclical phase will influence the profitability ranking. In the case of most bulk products, the real price development – where real price = inflation adjusted price – is declining by 0.5–2.0% per year. The speed of this trend depends on the technological development strategy of market leaders and other factors that add to future uncertainties.

2.3 Cost competitiveness

In addition to profitability and wood paying capacity, it is useful to analyse the cost competitiveness of any given project. The following two equations help determine cost competitiveness:

Sales price requirement = manufacturing cost + capital cost + transportation cost
Cash cost requirement = variable manufacturing cost + transportation cost

The concept of cost competitiveness includes the following features:
- No sales price estimates are necessary contrary to profitability and wood paying capacity analysis. This eliminates one uncertainty factor.
- In cost competitiveness comparisons of different regions, future exchange rate variations enter the picture. This is a factor of significant uncertainty.
- Cost competitiveness calculations usually use present cost and technology level. Future prediction of these factors gives the calculation greater accuracy.

CHAPTER 8

One can calculate cost competitiveness for new, hypothetical mills, using state-of-the-art technology as in Figure 4 or for existing mills or paper machines as in Figure 5[1].

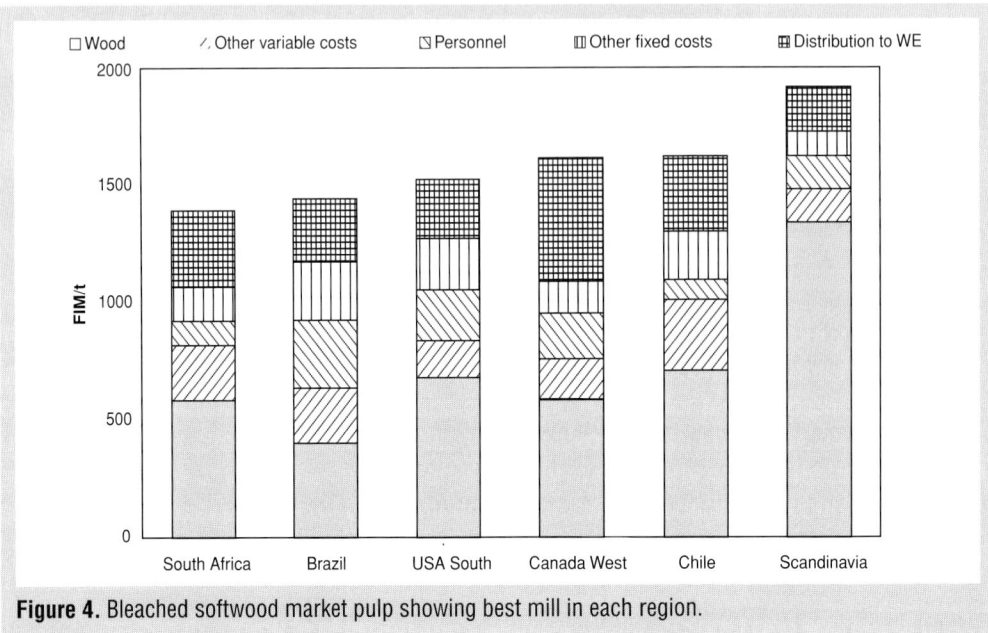

Figure 4. Bleached softwood market pulp showing best mill in each region.

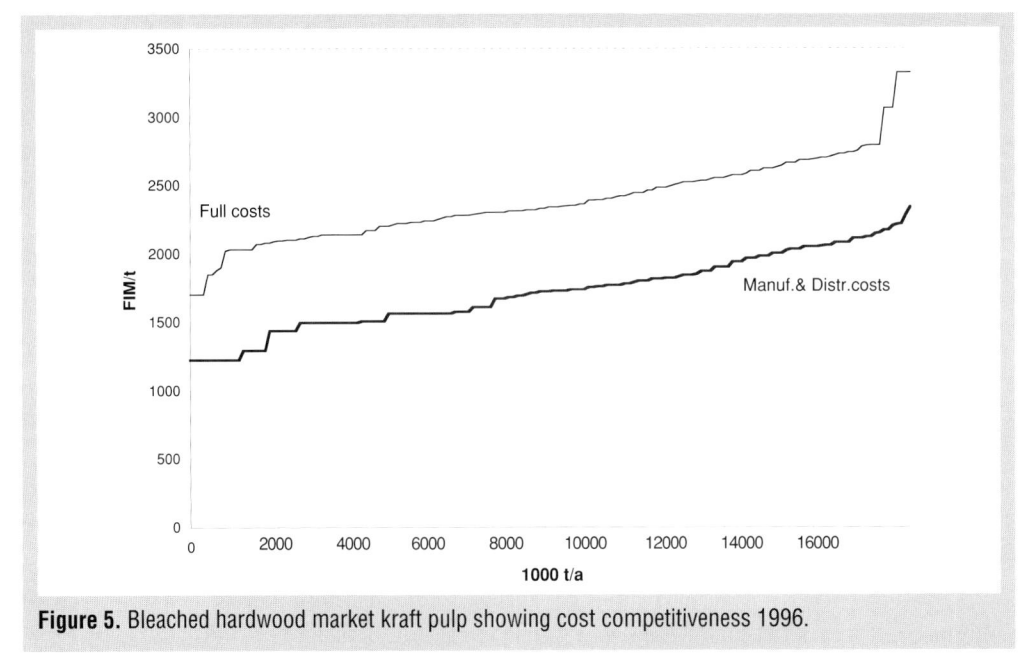

Figure 5. Bleached hardwood market kraft pulp showing cost competitiveness 1996.

The former analyses indicate the potential competitiveness of a region to produce a certain pulp or paper grade. The latter calculations indicate the present cost level and structure of existing producers.

Cost competitiveness analysis is used for the following purposes and in the following context:
1. The lowest cost producer is the price leader. If the market share of the price leader is sufficiently high, its producer can have a significant impact on overall price development.
2. During recessions when prices usually decrease, the bottom is often equal to the cash costs of the lowest cost producer. Prices do not dip beyond this point.
3. The cost curve structure of existing producers indicates many interesting factors that have an impact on the business climate. If the cost curve is steep – the difference between the highest and lowest cost producer is large – decreasing prices during recessions stop well ahead of the lowest cost producer's price. The reason is that high cost producers must stop production when the market price dips below their cash cost level. This helps to restore market and price balance. If the cost curve is flat – the difference between the highest and lowest cost producer is small – recession prices decline rapidly but stop at the lowest cash cost level or slightly above it.

It is obviously an advantage to participate as a low cost producer in a business where the cost curve is steep. This should theoretically make it possible to earn money in all phases of the cycle.

Figures 6 and 7 show that the importance of correct cost information in analysis of competitiveness is crucial.

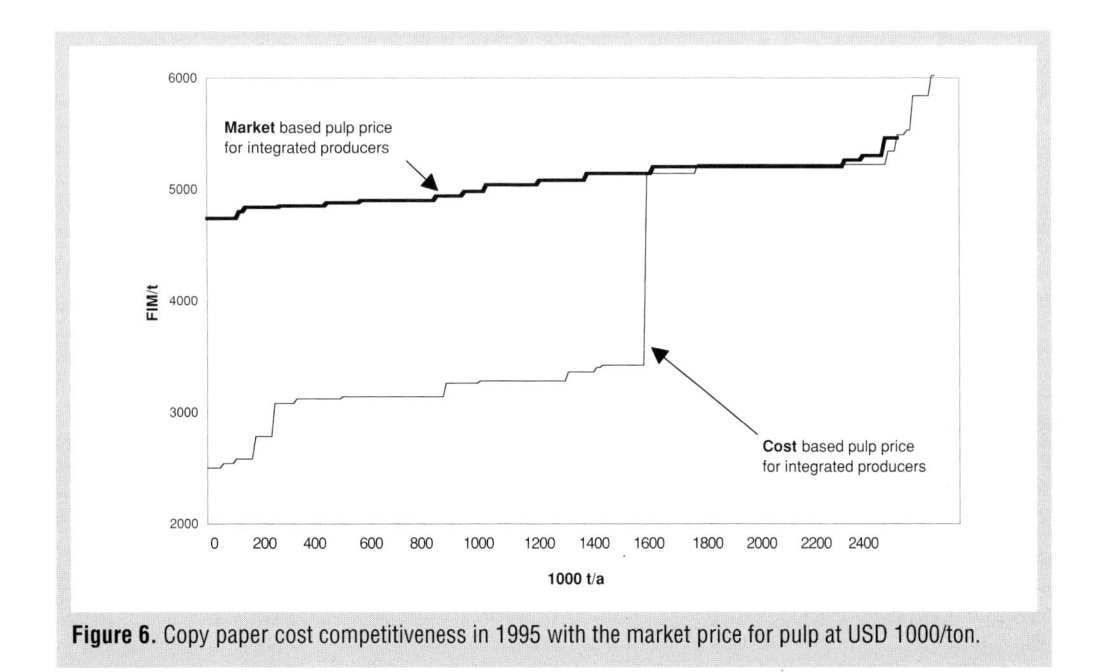

Figure 6. Copy paper cost competitiveness in 1995 with the market price for pulp at USD 1000/ton.

CHAPTER 8

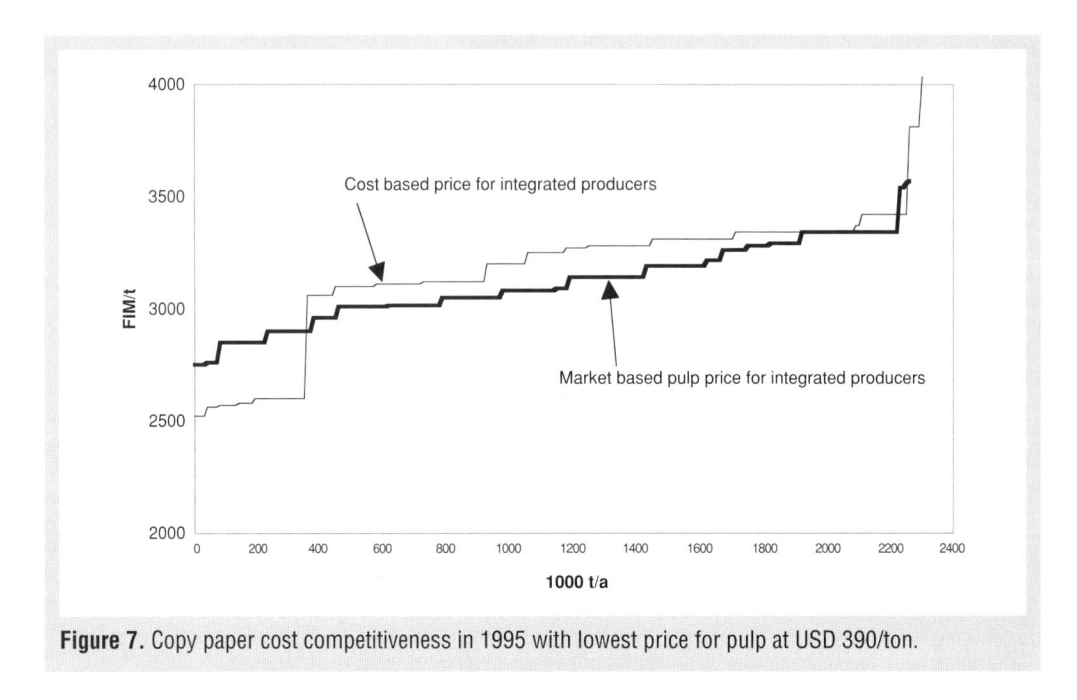

Figure 7. Copy paper cost competitiveness in 1995 with lowest price for pulp at USD 390/ton.

These exhibits illustrate the cash cost requirement of both integrated and nonintegrated producers of manufacturing copy paper using two market pulp prices.

Figure 6 indicates that the integrated producers have a huge competitive advantage. The high price of pulp that the nonintegrated producers must pay increases their cash costs to more than 50% above the level of the integrated producers.

Figure 7 illustrates the situation when pulp price is at its lowest level. The advantage of integration has turned into a slight cost disadvantage. Most of the integrated producers would have had lower costs, if they could have bought market pulp and shut down their own pulp mill.

3 Ability to take risks

According to the figures in Figure 1, cumulative capital outlay in a big project is at a maximum three years after the investment decision and one year after startup. This is the most critical time of the project. Considering the high debt burden and the internal costs associated with startup, a good startup with high production volume and high sales price of the product or good quality with favorable market conditions are necessary. Production volume and product quality are factors that are in the hands of the project team and influenced by well executed planning and implementation. Market conditions are an outside force that the project team cannot influence. They therefore remain an uncertainty and a risk factor.

An unfortunate development with Figure 1 would be the continued downward trend of the cumulative cash flow after the third year due to delay in implementation, technical problems, or poor market conditions. If the project financing has a high debt ratio, the situation for a small company quickly becomes critical. The size increase of new forest industry projects further aggravates the situation as Table 2 shows.

Table 2. Size of state-of-the-art forest industry projects at the end of 1996.

	Capacity t/a	Investment (mill.FIM / mill.USD)
Softwood chemical pulp	550 000	3600 / 780
Newsprint	280 000	2500 / 540
Lightweight coated	370 000	2700 / 590
Woodfree coated	360 000	2500 / 540
Woodfree uncoated	340 000	2000 / 430

1 USD = 4.6 FIM

To undertake any of the above projects, the size and financial strength of the company must be sufficient. A rough guideline is that the sales of the company should be at least 2–3 times the contemplated investment.

Table 3 analyzes the impact of inflation on risk.

Table 3. Impact of inflation on interest and amortization.

Debt	= 100		
Amortisation of debt 10 years	= 10/a		
	Case A	Case B	Case C
Interest rate X (%/a)	0	10	10
Inflation rate Y (%/a)	0	0	10
Real interest rate X-Y (%/a)	0	10	0
Year	Annual installments in year 1 money values		
1	10	20	18.2
2	10	19	15.7
3	10	18	13.5
4	10	17	11.6
5	10	16	9.9
6	10	15	8.5
7	10	14	7.2
8	10	13	6.1
9	10	12	6.1
10	10	11	4.2

As illustrated in the table, annual installments in the critical years immediately after startup do not significantly differ in cases B and C. Inflation has not yet had time to reduce the value of the investment. The impact of inflation in the first years is therefore

CHAPTER 8

small. It increases later to significant magnitude when it lowers the installments or capital costs considerably.

The inflation rate in the first half of the 1990s has been significantly lower in most countries compared with the level of the 1980s. Some countries have experienced negative inflation – deflation. The impact of inflation has been lower during the present decade. The low real interest rates that were a reality in some countries in the 1980s and earlier now seem to belong to history.

4 Selection criteria for new equipment

Selection criteria for new equipment should be based on the fact that manufacturing pulp and paper is a process consisting of a chain of equipment. When the chain is broken, the process stops.

Each machine and piece of equipment requires careful selection so the manufacturing process can perform properly and according to plan. The following aspects and criteria need consideration:

1. Performance and capacity
   The part having the lowest rate of production – the weakest link in the chain – determines the performance of the process. This part therefore requires rigorous analysis. The bottleneck of the process should be the most expensive machinery. In paper mills, this is usually the paper machine. In pulp mills, it is the recovery boiler.
2. Operational reliability
   The least reliable part of the process determines its total reliability. This is usually difficult to assess in advance. Conceptually, it consists of the probability of disturbances and breakdowns.
3. Maintenance
   This aspect requires that spare parts are easily available and that professional skills needed for maintenance exist at the mill or are readily available nearby. Standardization of electrical motors, bearings, etc. is an advantage in ensuring proper maintenance.
4. Controlability
   The process should be easy to control. Relevant measurements should be readily available to adjust the process or machine in the direction desired. Reliable repeatability is an important factor.
5. Guarantees
   Most deliveries contain a guarantee clause that includes a penalty if delivery is late or does not perform according to standard. Note that penalties can never be sufficiently high to compensate the buyer for lost production. For instance, a one-day shut-down for a new pulp mill means approximately FIM 1.5 million lost contribution at USD 640/ton pulp price.
   Guarantees and penalties are a way of assuring the cooperation of suppliers in correcting possible malfunctions and deficiencies in deliveries.

6. Price

   The price is an important factor. Considering the above facts, it is not a decisive aspect of selection criteria. Price alone should never be the sole basis for selection.

   Analyzing the costs of a large forest industry project can substantiate the above statement.

   Table 4. Cost breakdown of a large forest industry project.

		Share %
1	Main process equipment	29
2	Auxiliary equipment, material for piping and tanks	11
3	Electrical and instrumentation	9
4	Insulation, paint etc.	2
5	Construction management	6
6	Engineering	5
7	Erection	15
8	Civil works	20
9	Insurance, freight, others	3
10	TOTAL	100

   Table 4 shows that the share of main process equipment in total investment cost is less than 30%. A 10% savings in this item will lower the total investment cost less than 3%. As Figure 2 shows, the change of total investment costs does not influence the profitability of a project to any appreciable degree. A 3% reduction in investment cost improves the IRR by less than one percentage unit in Figure 2.

   An example of the conclusions drawn from Table 4 are projects where a new paper machine is installed in an old building. Provided that the existing infrastructure allows maximum use of economy of scale, such a project is often successful. Savings can be achieved with items 2–9 in Table 4 comprising two-thirds of project costs.

   A contrary example is a case where an old paper machine is installed in a new building. The savings can only come from item 1 in Table 4 forming less than one-third of the investment cost. An old machine cannot achieve the performance level of a new one. There will always be low production that will have a detrimental effect on profitability.

7. References

   Many of the above aspects are difficult to substantiate. One must trust in the suppliers' good references and earlier experience.

CHAPTER 9

Economy of scale

1. Description and definition 141
2. Economy of scale of a pulp mill 142
3. Economy of scale of a paper mill 144
4. Minimill concept 146
5. Economy of scale of speciality paper mills 147
6. Future development of economy of scale 148
   Sources... 150

CHAPTER 9

Economy of scale

1 Description and definition

The size of new paper machines and pulp mills has increased constantly during the last 30–40 years.

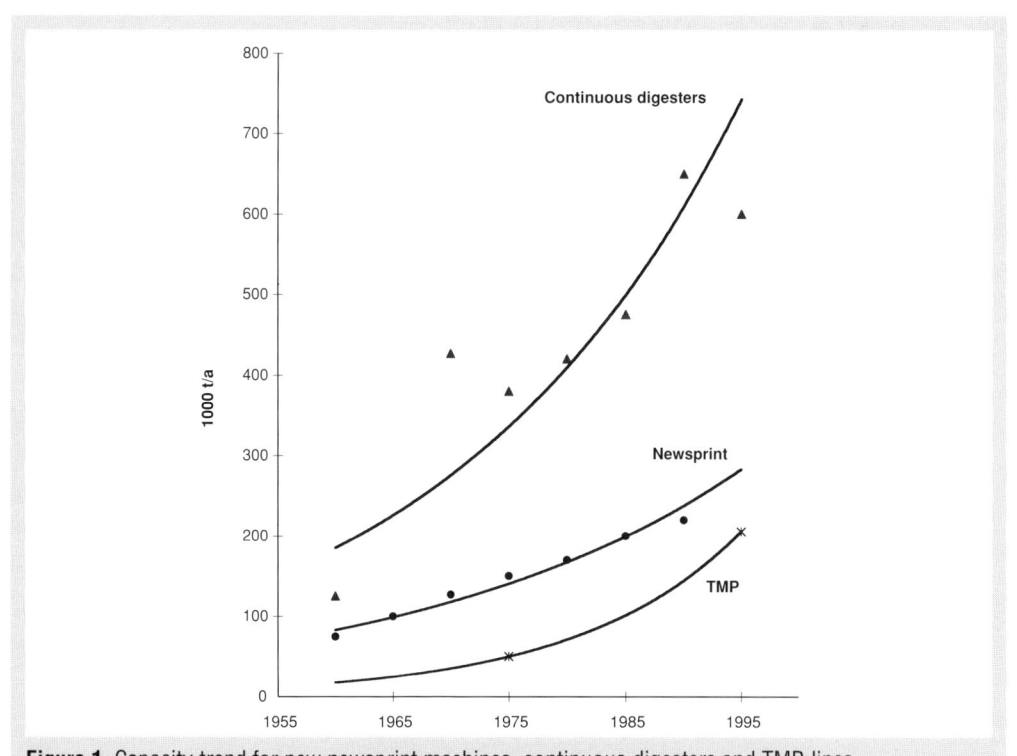

Figure 1. Capacity trend for new newsprint machines, continuous digesters and TMP-lines.

As illustrated in Figure 1, the size of new newsprint machines has increased from 75 000 tons/year to 280 000 tons/year – a factor of approximately 4 – during 1960–1995[1]. This means an annual increase of 4%. The growth in size for continuous digesters has been even faster at 5% per year[3].

The main reasons for the increase in size have been the lower investment and manufacturing costs per ton of output attained through larger unit size.

Economy of scale can therefore be defined as follows:

> Economy of scale is the cost advantage achieved by using large and growing unit sizes in the manufacturing process.

CHAPTER 9

The following general characteristics apply to economy of scale:
- The investment cost per ton of a large unit such as a pulp line or paper machine is lower than for a similar unit of small or medium size.
- Manufacturing costs per ton of output are often lower in a large unit. For example, wages and salaries might be numerically on the same level regardless of the size of a new line, because the number of personnel is the same. However, due to larger output, the costs per ton are lower for the large unit.

There is an upper limit for new machinery that restricts the output to a certain maximum. Exceeding this limit initiates a two line solution. Some savings can still be achieved in such a situation, although the advantages tend to stabilize at a certain level. Typical savings achieved in these cases are the following:
- mill area and infrastructure such as railway, roads, maintenance departments, administration buildings, water intake, effluent treatment, etc.
- general overhead including administration, health care, research and development, etc.

The minimum economical size of a line is the size after which the cost advantage of larger capacity becomes minimal. In time, this size on most grades increases. As a general rule for bulk grades such as pulp, newsprint, woodfree and woodcontaining printing papers, kraftliner, etc. building a new line that is of maximum size or close to it is necessary to use economy of scale to the utmost.

With the maximum size of a line increasing with time, it has become apparent that large size also has disadvantages:
- the availability of raw material such as wood or recovered paper cannot be reasonably secure due to the large volumes necessary
- transportation of raw material such as wood or recovered paper occurs over a wider area causing increased costs
- the environmental load increases to an unsatisfactory level
- small orders are difficult to produce efficiently
- marketing efforts must cover a wider geographical area. This adds marketing costs and increases transportation costs of finished products (= lowers sales price at the mill).

The above factors are becoming critical in many instances especially when considering new mill sites.

2 Economy of scale of a pulp mill

Economy of scale in a pulp mill is determined by the main machinery, such as digesters, recovery boiler, and pulp drying machine. In most cases, economy of scale is significant for investment and manufacturing costs. The largest size is therefore usually selected especially when building new mills. In 1995, the largest single line operations had a capacity of 600 000 tons/year. According to existing proposed investment plans, this figure will probably increase to 800 000 tons/year before the end of the century.

If a production figure higher than indicated above is necessary, a two line solution is necessary. Figure 2 shows the effect of economy of scale on profitability as a function of capacity in Scandinavia, Indonesia, and Brazil.

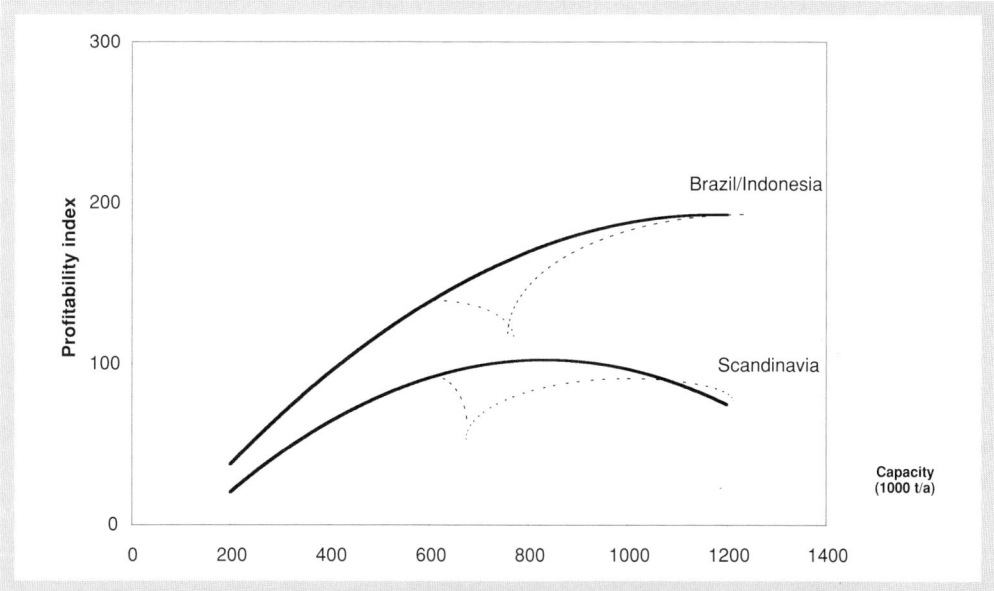

Figure 2. Profitability as a function of capacity in a Scandinavian, Brazilian, and Indonesian kraft pulp mill.

- In Scandinavia, the figure indicates that a second pulp line does not add to profitability. The main reason for this is higher wood costs due to longer transportation distances causing higher transportation costs for the raw material.
- In Brazil and Indonesia, a second pulp line adds to economy of scale – improves profitability, because investments in infrastructure including railroads, roads, bleaching chemical and electricity supply, housing for employees, etc., are very high for the first pulp line. In Scandinavia, most of the infrastructure exists and does not require any additional investment. Accordingly the investment costs for the first line are lower in Scandinavia and approximately at the same level as the investment costs of a second line in Brazil and Indonesia.
- The profitability of a new pulp line in Brazil or Indonesia is as good or better than in Scandinavia due to lower wood costs. The rapid growth of wood in these regions ensures that the second line does not significantly add to wood transportation and costs as Table 1 shows.

Table 1. Wood growth area comparison in Brazil between 600 000 and 1 200 000 t/a kraft pulp mill.

	Case A	Case B
Production (t/a)	600 000	1 200 000
Wood consumption (m^3/t)	4	4
Wood consumption (million m^3/a)	2.4	4.8
Wood growth (m^3/ha / a)	30	30
Area required for wood supply growth (ha) growth (km x km)	80 000 30 x 30	160 000 40 x 40

Although the example in the table is simplified, it illustrates the need for only a small additional wood transportation distance for the second line. The advantage of lower wood costs remains. Combined with equal investment costs, this gives Brazil and Indonesia a clear advantage.

3 Economy of scale of a paper mill

The speed and width of its paper machine influence the economy of scale of a paper mill. The dominant factor since the early 1980s has been speed rather than width. In bulk grades, a machine wire width of 9–10 m was possible during the 1970s. This is still the maximum width due to the following factors:
- Roll diameter increases by an exponential factor of three causing dramatic increases with higher widths. Increased weight and price will result.
- The manufacturing machinery including grinders and foundry of the principal paper machine builders such as Valmet, Voith, and Beloit have had a limit of approximately 10 m.
- The manufacturing machinery of wire and felt manufacturers have also restricted them to 10 m.

Economy of scale

Figure 3 shows that the development of economy of scale through speed has been dramatic[1].

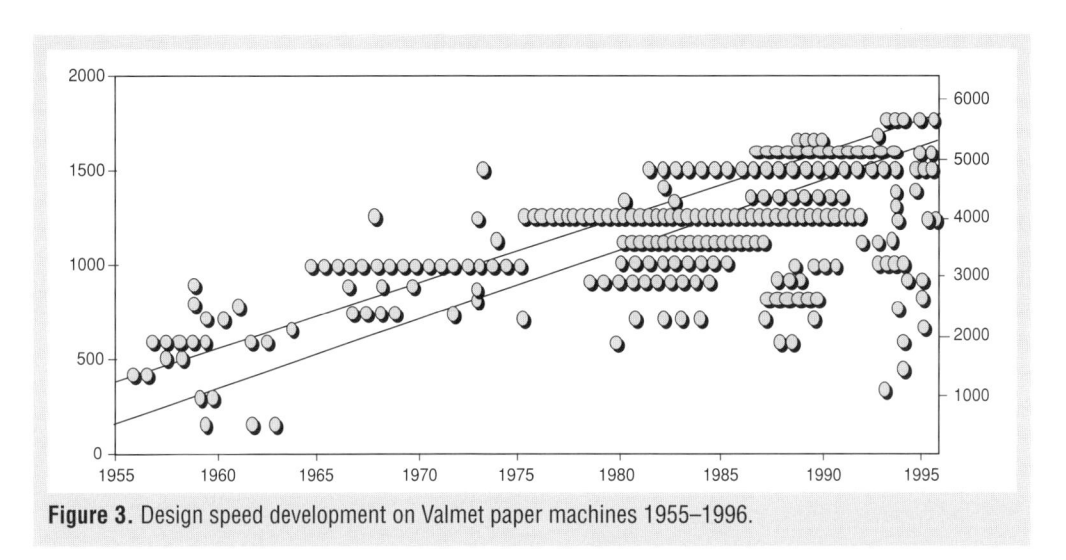

Figure 3. Design speed development on Valmet paper machines 1955–1996.

The maximum speed on new newsprint machines in 1955 was approximately 400 m/min. In 1995, it had increased by a factor of four to 1600 m/min. This is an annual increase of 3.5% or 30 m/min.

The use of higher widths than the present maximum of 9–10 m seems unlikely although not impossible due to construction and technical constraints. Research and development efforts therefore concentrate primarily on increasing the paper machine speeds limited by process technology. Maximum paper machine speeds will therefore probably continue to grow at an accelerating rate.

To use the future potential economy of scale from paper machine speed increases, the maximum speed of the drive should usually be slightly higher – for example 100 m/min – than the maximum running speed with best available technology (BAT). The balancing speed of the rolls in the paper machine should also exceed the drive speed by another 100 m/min. The additional costs of these measures are negligible compared with total project costs.

The paper machine alone constitutes 20–25% of the total mill investment. Economy of scale for the entire project can sometimes increase further at capacity levels where economy of scale for the paper machine alone is decreasing.

Economy of scale in two line paper mills

The addition of a second paper machine in a single paper machine installation always improves the economy of scale. The reason for this is that the investment costs for the second line are 10–20% lower than for the first line due to the savings with existing infrastructure. Another benefit is the experience from the first installation in startup, marketing, etc.

CHAPTER 9

When selecting a greenfield site for a new paper mill, the location should therefore allow for building at least a second paper machine. In many cases, a third and fourth paper machine on the same site will have the same benefits as the second machine. A greenfield site that allows for building three or four paper machines could offer an attractive alternative. Space, layouts, water availability, energy, environmental factors, etc., require consideration for a much larger production than that for only one machine when selecting a greenfield site.

4 Minimill concept

The use of economy of scale has been a dominant factor when building new pulp and paper mills during the last decades. Disadvantages connected with large production units can include the following:
- high total investment risk and therefore increased financial risk
- higher total environmental loads
- the exclusion of excellent mill locations suitable for small to medium size mills only due to restriction in water availability, total area available, etc.

The increased use of recycled fiber has developed new ideas that sometimes run contrary to economy of scale. Recycled fiber is readily available near large paper consumption sites such as large cities. Therefore a paper mill located close to its raw material source – a population center – would have minimum transportation distance and costs for its raw material and maybe even the end product. Although the location of a paper mill near a population center can therefore offer certain advantages, suitable paper machine sites are seldom available for large units near cities. With the new technologies that lower water consumption and waste per ton of output, a small to medium size mill could be near its raw material source – a city.

The advantages of the minimill concept are the following:
- smaller total investment and total risk
- proximity to raw material source and markets means lower raw material costs and increased product price at the mill due to lower transportation costs
- possibility of using existing infrastructures such as energy supply source from a municipal power station, effluent treatment at a municipal sewage system, railroads, roads, etc., to lower investment costs
- good availability of high quality personnel
- use of maintenance facilities outside the mill, but in its physical proximity
- simpler technology provides a larger number of equipment suppliers than for BAT machines with more intense competition to lower total investment costs.

Some disadvantages also exist:
- investment costs per ton of output are difficult to keep at an equal or lower level compared with large units
- production costs despite advantages enumerated earlier are difficult to keep on an equal or lower level than with large units because manpower costs per ton of output are higher since the number of personnel is the same regardless of unit size

The minimills contemplated in the 1990s are usually 2.5–5 m wide. This is often a multiple of the most common corrugator widths. The production capacity is 60 000–150 000 tons/year. These mills produce bulk products such as corrugating raw materials including testliner and wellenstoff. They are therefore meant to compete on an equal footing with large producers of similar grades.

5 Economy of scale of speciality paper mills

As specified earlier in this book, the single most important buying criterion for bulk products such as newsprint, corrugating raw materials, etc., is price. Low manufacturing costs are therefore critical. For speciality papers, quality, service, research and development support, etc., are becoming more important. These factors can often overshadow the price aspect as buying criteria. As a result, large machines do not produce speciality papers, and use of economy of scale as a competition factor is rare.

If a speciality grade develops over time into a bulk grade, the competitive environment changes radically. This happened in the 1970s with uncoated fine papers and in the 1980s with coated fine papers. These grades had been nonstandard specialities ordered and produced to specific customer requirements. Volume was often small. This caused small production runs and frequent quality changes that would have ruined the efficiency and profitability of large machines. As a result, fine papers were produced on 2–4 meter wide machines with capacities of 10 000–30 000 tons/year. Some fine papers such as printing and writing paper, continuous stationery, and bulk offset have now become standard allowing the use of economy of scale as a competitive factor. New machines built after 1985 have therefore had maximum width and speed with a production capacity of 200 000–350 000 tons/year.

Many speciality paper grades have low market volumes. These include bible paper, cable paper, cigarette paper, filter papers for the automotive industry, wet strength label paper, teabag paper, four-color copy paper, etc. Manufacturing these grades on small paper machines can be highly profitable despite the short production runs and frequent grade changes that can cause low efficiency and production rates on a larger paper machine. High paper price caused by successful tailoring of quality to meet customer specifications is the key success factor, rather than low manufacturing costs caused by efficient production.

The optimum size of a speciality paper machine can be calculated on the basis of order size, estimated time required for grade change, total estimated production volume according to market size for main grades, etc. Benchmarking by utilizing the experience

CHAPTER 9

of existing machines gives additional information which is of value in determining the optimum machine size.

6 Future development of economy of scale

Economy of scale will probably increase the maximum size of both pulp mills and paper machines in the future.

The maximum size of single line pulp mills with continuous digesters is likely to increase from 600 000 tons/year in the middle 1990s to 800 000 tons/year by the end of the century, assuming that recovery boilers and drying machines can provide a corresponding capacity increase. For batch digesters, the recovery boiler and drying machine will be the limiting factors, since increasing the number of digesters is easy.

The maximum width of paper machines is not likely to increase from the present 9–10 m. However, maximum speed will continue to increase. For newsprint, SC, and LWC papers, the present maximum speed of 1500–1600 m/min will approach 1800 m/min by the end of the century with a resulting increase in production capacity.

An interesting problem is the necessity and viability of using maximum economy of scale in the future on bulk grades. Figure 4 is an attempt to provide a solution to this problem.

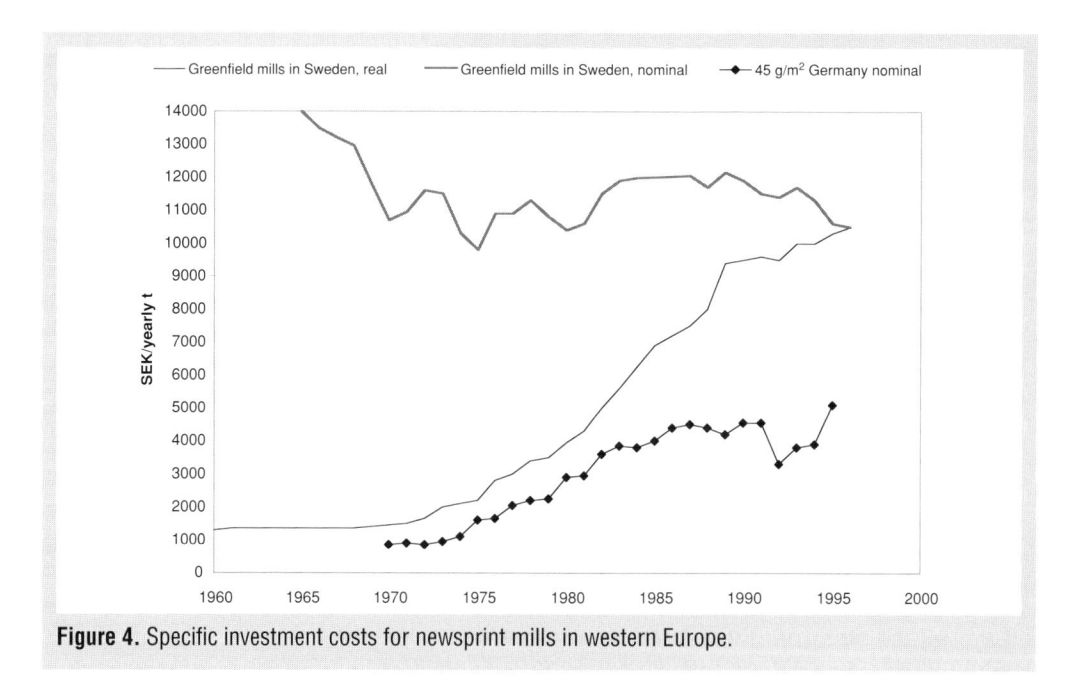

Figure 4. Specific investment costs for newsprint mills in western Europe.

In Figure 4, the capacity of new newsprint machines has increased from 130 000 tons/year in 1970 to 280 000 tons/year in 1995. The investment cost per ton of annual output in real terms has been fairly constant at 10 000–12 000 SEK/ton. No clear downward trend is visible. The nominal investment costs per ton of output have increased from 1 900 SEK/ton to 11 000 SEK/ton during 1970–1995. This is approximately 9% per year. At the same time, newsprint prices have increased in nominal terms from 800 SEK/ton to 5 000 SEK/ton. This is 7% per year. Investment costs despite economy of scale have risen faster than output lowering the margin – price less capital costs.

The only way to compensate for this and maintain profitability is by lowering manufacturing costs such as raw material, energy, personnel, and other fixed costs. Since many of these costs have risen faster than nominal prices – personnel and energy unit costs in particular, pressure to reduce these through lower unit consumption and higher efficiency has been great.

The above example indicates that not using economy of scale to the utmost puts an investment at a disadvantage. Its use is therefore likely. In the future, this is an additional driving force for machinery builders to continue their efforts to develop more efficient machinery. Such interest is a prerequisite for the continued use of economy of scale.

Two line pulp mills with capacities over one million tons per year will probably not be viable in Scandinavia due to the lack of wood or the prohibitive wood costs caused by high transportation costs. This will further reduce the competitiveness of Scandinavian pulp producers compared with countries with rapidly growing forests.

CHAPTER 9

Sources

1   Valmet
2   Sprout-Waldron
3   Kvaerner Pulping
4   Jaakko Pöyry Consulting Oy

CHAPTER 10

Economy of integration

1	Definitions	152
2	Financial integration	152
3	Vertical integration	153
4	Optimized multiproduct integration in Scandinavia	156
5	Two common development strategies of the forest industry	157
	Sources	158

CHAPTER 10

Economy of integration

1 Definitions

Integration means the operation of several manufacturing locations and mills under common leadership and management. Various types of integration are possible:
- financial integration means cooperation between geographically separated units based on common ownership
- vertical integration means that the end product of one manufacturing unit forms the raw material of another. Examples would be a pulp mill producing pulp for a paper mill, a saw mill producing chips for a TMP plant, etc.
- in horizontal integration, different units use the same raw material base. A saw mill and a pulp mill are examples
- geographical integration means cooperation between different units located in close geographical proximity. They are usually on the same mill site.
- Optimum multiproduct integration refers to geographically integrated units combined to use raw materials such as the wood resources of a certain area in the best way.

The aim of integration is to achieve benefits and savings not obtainable without integration.

2 Financial integration

Financial integration has been a dominant feature in the forest industry during the second half of the 1980s and the first half of the 1990s. The main objectives of financial integration are as follows:
1. More efficient use of investment funds by using economy of scale and directing investments to those geographical areas and locations that have the highest earning potential
2. Lessening the impact of cyclical variations mainly caused by the following three factors:
    - economic fluctuations in the national economy causing changes in competitiveness and the profitability of manufacturing in that country or region
    - variations in the demand for a certain paper grade
    - economic fluctuations in a larger geographical region such as Europe influencing the overall demand pattern of forest products.

The impact of cyclical variations can be decreased with financial integration by spreading the risk of market areas and manufacturing locations.

3. Improving efficiency of operations by streamlining production. A typical way to achieve this is to limit the number of grades of each paper machine or production unit rather than having each production unit produce a wide variety of grades. Such specialization improves production efficiency by several percent without requiring any investments. Certain additional quality improvements such as a more stable quality level can also be achieved. The example of Table 1 illustrates the potential benefits of these measures.

Table 1. Impact of production streamlining on profitability.

Two paper companies, each with a yearly newsprint production of 450 000 tons, income of 105, variable costs 49.3 and fixed costs of 50.7, decide to merge. After the merger production is streamlined which increases the total production by 5% or 22 500		
1. Income	1.05 x 105	= 110.25
2. Variable costs	1.05 x 49.3	= 51.77
3. Fixed costs		= 50.7
4. Profit		= 7.78
5. Profit with 450 000 t/a production		= 5
6. Difference (4) - (5)		= 2.78

The extra profit of 2.78 gained in the table is significant. Its capitalized value – its present value assuming a constant extra profit of 2.78 during a reasonable period of time such as 5 years – varies with the interest rate and number of years between 15–20. For a 450 000 tons/year newsprint mill, this equals approximately USD 50–65 million in extra value.

3 Vertical integration

The main characteristics of vertical integration are the following:
- achieving higher value added production
- increasing sales without increasing raw material consumption
- changing the mode of operation to a marketing orientation so that production and raw material oriented policies are less important.

Table 2 gives a typical example of the development from raw material to market oriented operation by showing the steps in the development of a company through vertical integration.

CHAPTER 10

Table 2. Development from raw material to market oriented operation.

Development from raw material to market oriented operation	
Step 1	Sales of wood and woodchips
Step 2	Sale of pulp
Step 3	Sale of liquid packaging board
Step 4	Sale of polyethylene coated liquid packaging board
Step 5	Sale of liquid packages
Step 6	Sale of packaging systems

In the table, step 1 is totally raw material oriented, and step 6 is totally market oriented.

Vertical geographical integration makes it possible to achieve integration benefits impossible to obtain in production facilities located in different sites.
- some manufacturing phases are eliminated, saving both capital and costs. For example, pulp drying and baling is unnecessary in an integrated pulp and fine paper manufacturing plant. The savings are approximately FIM 100–200/ton or 5–10% of pulp manufacturing costs
- in a converting plant integrated in a paper mill such as a sheeting plant in a fine paper mill, the paper mill can reuse the broke from the converting plant
- it is also possible to use economy of scale more efficiently. An example would be using the energy generated by the production process. This lowers both investment and production costs.

Vertical geographical integration is often limited and not feasible for market reasons. Particularly high value-added products require production near their markets. This often requires cutting the vertical integration geographically.

A typical question facing all Scandinavian pulp and fine paper mills concerns the most feasible location of paper and sheeting production in Europe. Table 3 shows three possible alternatives.

Table 3. Feasible locations of paper and sheeting production in Europe.

	Alternative 1	Alternative 2	Alternative 3
Scandinavia	Pulp production Paper production Sheeting	Pulp production Paper production	Pulp
Central Europe		Sheeting	Paper production Sheeting

All alternatives in the table are feasible under certain circumstances, and all have been implemented at some time. Tables 4–6 show the advantages and disadvantages of each alternative.

Table 4. Alternative 1.

Alternative 1: Pulp, paper and sheeting manufacture is geographically integrated to one site in Scandinavia, sheets are shipped to central Europe	
Advantages	**Disadvantages**
+ manufacturing cost savings through elimination of pulp drying	- longer delivery time of sheeted products in comparison to sheeting facility located in Europe
+ capital cost saving through elimination of pulp drying and baling	- more transport damages of sheeted products in comparison to
+ capital cost saving through smaller energy generation unit (energy of pulp dryer is used on paper machine)	1. Sheeting facility in central Europe 2. Pulp bales or paper rolls produced alternatively
+ sheeting broke re-used at paper mill without storage and transport	- relatively higher transport costs of sheeted products in comparison to pulp bales or paper rolls
+ control of total manufacturing chain at one single location	- larger storage capacity and thus working capital requirements to compensate for longer delivery time
	- longer distance to end user and consequently less communication

Table 5. Alternative 2.

Alternative 2: Pulp and paper is geographically integrated to one site in Scandinavia Reels are shipped to central Europe	
Advantages	**Disadvantages**
+ capital cost savings through elimination of pulp drying and baling	- not possible to re-use sheeted broke on same site
+ capital cost saving through smaller energy generation unit (energy of pulp dryer is used by paper machine)	- integration of production planning with paper mill more complicated than in Alternative 1
+ manufacturing cost savings through elimination of pulp drying	- longer distance and less communication to paper mill
+ short delivery time of sheeted products	- need for larger intermediate storage of reels and consequently higher working capital in order to achieve short delivery time of sheets and production runs of suitable length on the paper machine
+ short distance and easy communication with end user	

Table 6. Alternative 3.

Alternative 3: Pulp mill located in Scandinavia and pulp shipped in bales to central Europe Paper production and sheeting integrated at one site in central Europe	
Advantages	Disadvantages
+ short delivery time for sheeted products	- higher capital costs due to pulp drying and baling
+ short distance and easy communication with end user	- higher capital costs due to two separate energy units (pulp mill and paper mill)
+ sheeting broke re-used at paper mill without storage and transport	- higher manufacturing costs due to pulpdrying
+ integration of production planning with paper mill	
+ possibility to use pulp from other sources also	

The selection of any possible alternative requires careful analysis. The existing structure – present production facilities – requires consideration, since integration benefits through expansion might provide additional savings. Note that all the alternatives are practicable, depending on circumstances.

4 Optimized multiproduct integration in Scandinavia

The purpose of multiproduct integration is to use a limited volume of wood raw material in the best way. Since wood is the limiting factor, the decisive criterion is the wood paying capacity for different wood species and different log sizes – fiber wood and logs.

Research from the late 1960s produces the following conclusions for Scandinavian circumstances[1]:
1. Optimum economy of scale with a total wood consumption of 3 million m³/year.
2. Birch logs should be processed to plywood.
3. Pine and spruce logs should be processed to sawn goods and the chips to chemical pulp or TMP for spruce.
4. Spruce fiber wood should be processed to mechanical pulp and then into paper.
5. Pine and birch fiber wood should be processed to chemical pulp and then into paper.

The existing industry essentially uses all the wood resources in Scandinavia. A new, multiproduct integrate consuming 3 million m³/year would require a significant restructuring including shut-downs of the existing industry. Since this is unlikely, a new multiproduct integrate in Scandinavia now or in the future must be considered purely hypothetical. When planning the future of existing plants, the structure of the multiproduct integrated organization could serve as a model to direct the total development.

5 Two common development strategies of the forest industry

Considering the description of different integration alternatives, the following fundamentally different development strategies may be formulated.
1. Increase of added value based on vertical integration.
2. Multiproduct integrated organization with optimum use of wood raw material.

The main characteristics and fundamental differences of these two strategies are summarised below.

Table 7. Two forest industry development strategies.

	Forest industry development strategies	
	Vertical integration	**Multiproduct integrate**
Strategic base	Increase of add-on value	Optimal use of wood raw-material
End products	Specialities	Bulk products
Mode of operation	Market oriented	Raw material and production oriented
Raw material	Dependency on wood raw material decreases	Use of wood raw material is optimized
Industry structure	Decentralized, international	Located close to raw material sources
Limiting factor of operation	Markets, integration of add-on value products to unprofitable products does not improve competitiveness sufficiently	Availability of wood limits growth

The application of both these strategies simultaneously in one company is difficult and usually not very successful. Considering the increasing size of the Scandinavian forest companies with the probable lack of raw material in the future, the following scenarios may be possible:
1. A multiproduct integrated organization produces bulk products in an efficient and optimal way.
2. At a later stage when availability of wood raw material is a limitation, growth is generated through market oriented vertical integration. This can use self-manufactured bulk products.

CHAPTER 10

Sources

1   Ryti, Kirjasniemi: Paperi ja Puu No. 3 (1968)

CHAPTER 11

The impact of currency exchange rates on competitiveness

1	**Introduction**	**160**
2	**Definitions**	**160**
2.1	Balance of trade and current balance	160
2.2	Inflation	161
2.3	Purchasing power parity and currency adjustments	161
3	**Historical aspects of the western monetary system**	**162**
4	**Factors affecting exchange rates**	**164**
5	**Purchasing power parity**	**165**
6	**Conclusions**	**169**
7	**Protective measures against exchange rate variations**	**170**
7.1	General	170
7.2	Structure of currency position	170
7.3	Forward selling and buying	171

CHAPTER 11

The impact of currency exchange rates on competitiveness

1 Introduction

The Scandinavian companies especially export most of their forest industry production. Their costs are therefore in domestic currency, and their sales revenues are predominantly in some foreign currency. As a result, fluctuations in exchange rates between seller and buyer countries immediately influence the net result.

When two companies located in different countries compete for an order in a third country, exchange rate variations between the countries influence the competitive position of both companies. As explained in Chapter 8, section 2.3, exchange rate variations are the largest uncertainty factor in analysis of competition.

Since exchange rate variations have such a significant effect on the forest industry, this chapter clarifies some basic principles of international finance and its impact on forest industry operations.

2 Definitions

2.1 Balance of trade and current balance

In all countries, a central bank controls the currency flow. When a foreign buyer pays for purchased goods in his domestic currency such as DEM or USD, this increases the currency reserve of the central bank of the receiving country. The central bank then pays the producer of the goods in the domestic currency. Exports therefore increase the currency reserve and flow of domestic currency of the exporting country.

When a domestic company buys foreign goods, it pays the central bank in its domestic currency. The central bank uses its currency reserve to pay in foreign currency to the producer of the purchased goods. Therefore imports decrease the currency reserve and the flow of domestic currency of the importing country.

The balance of trade is calculated on the amount and value of goods exported and imported during a given period of time. The definition is as follows:

Balance of trade = value of merchandise exports − value of merchandise imports

If the balance of trade includes intangible factors such as services, tourism, etc., a current balance or current account is formed. It has the following definition:

Current balance = value of all exports (merchandise and services)
− value of all imports (merchandise and services)
+ net receipts of interest, profits, and dividends from abroad.

The current balance or current account therefore also equals the sum of visible (trade) and invisible balances. A country that has a positive current balance accumulates more currencies than it consumes.

2.2 Inflation

Inflation is the decrease in purchasing power of the domestic currency. According to modern monetary theory, inflation is the outcome of an expansion of the money supply in excess of real output growth. In practice, inflation has the following effects:
- the domestic price level increases
- due to higher price level the cost competitiveness in relation to competing countries decreases. This lowers exports and the currency reserve
- the competitiveness of imports increases so that the volume of imports grows and lowers the currency reserve.

A high inflation rate compared with competing countries therefore causes the currency reserve to decrease. If this development continues, it forces the central bank to take steps to strengthen the domestic currency. A commonly used measure to counteract this trend is increasing the domestic interest rate. This causes higher savings rate and less consumption, both of domestic and imported goods. Investments also decline as a result of the higher cost of borrowed capital. This measure often causes the unemployment rate to rise.

A second measure often used to correct the negative effects of a high inflation rate is currency adjustment as described below.

2.3 Purchasing power parity and currency adjustments

In theory, exchange adjusted prices of identical tradable goods must be equal globally. This concept is known as the law of one price. For this to happen, the foreign exchange rate must change by the difference between the domestic and foreign rate of inflation. This relationship is called purchasing power parity. In simple terms, it means that a unit of domestic currency should have the same purchasing power around the world. Because of different inflation rates, exchange rate corrections should equalize purchasing power in different countries.

Devaluation means lowering the exchange rate in relation to foreign currencies. It has the following effects:
- The competitiveness of the domestic industry improves thereby increasing exports and the currency reserve.
- Imports become more expensive. This usually lowers the volume of imports and the demand on the currency reserve.
- The input of imports for domestic production increases in price.
- Foreign debt becomes instantaneously more expensive. This is the case for both interest payments and amortization.
- The inflation rate often, but not always, increases.

Devaluation increases the cost of living due to higher prices on imported goods and services, foreign travel, etc. Devaluation therefore means a decline in the total salary level and the standard of living. This causes new pressure for wage increases and higher costs of domestic raw material such as wood. It may trigger a new round of inflation and subsequent currency exchange movements.

Revaluation is the opposite of devaluation. It means increase of the exchange rate in relation to foreign currencies. Revaluation can be effective if a country has an excessively high currency reserve and the competitiveness of the domestic industry is good. As the price level of imports declines, revaluation causes an overall increase in the standard of living.

3 Historical aspects of the western monetary system

After World War II, the western monetary system used the Bretton Woods agreement containing the following main points:
1. The value of USD was tied to gold with one ounce of gold at USD 35.
2. All other currencies were tied to USD and therefore indirectly to gold. Exchange rates between currencies were fixed with the limits of currency movements at ±1%.
3. As a result of the above factors, USD became a reserve currency kept by most other countries in their currency reserves in the 1950s and 1960s. This arrangement was considered to be safe, since dollars could always be exchanged for gold if necessary.

The fixed exchange rates stipulated in the Bretton Woods agreement functioned well until the beginning of the 1970s During that period currency fluctuations between major countries were rare. The United States ran a constant current account deficit that the reserves of other central banks absorbed. If a country had a severe imbalance in its economy for a long period or a higher inflation rate in relation to other countries with a resultant dangerous decline in its currency reserve, a devaluation of this currency occurred in agreement with the International Monetary Fund (IMF).

At the end of the 1960s, the inflation rate in the United States increased due partly to the Vietnam war. As a result, the volume of USD increased to such an extent that its exchange for gold became unrealistic. For this reason, the exhange of USD to gold ended in 1968 for private persons. Finally, in 1971 during the Nixon administration, the exchange of USD for gold stopped entirely. Simultaneously, the USD was devalued by 10% against other currencies.

Western monetary policies still aimed at maintaining fixed exchange rates as earlier, but this proved to be impossible. In March 1973, major currencies started to float with their exchange rate determined by supply and demand. This meant a dramatic change.

In 1972, the most important European countries agreed to allow their currencies to move ± 1.125% from the average value. This system was known as the European currency snake and formed the basis of the European Monetary System (EMS) implemented in 1979. The EMS had three main elements:
- Exchange Rate Mechanism (ERM) with all member countries' currencies fixed to the European Currency Unit (ECU) with movement limits of ± 2.25%
- ECU was the average basket value of its member countries
- intervention mechanisms.

When first implemented, the EMS did not work as planned and several currency adjustments were necessary as countries with high inflation rates had to devaluate. The EMS system did gradually stabilize so that between 1987 and 1992 there were no devaluations or revaluations of member countries' currencies. After 1992, the stability between currencies again deteriorated resulting in a ±15% limit to currency movements after August 1993.

During the 1990s, the major developmental influence on economy and exchange rate fluctuations was the formation of the European Economic and Monetary Union, based on the Maastricht Treaty of February 1992. All European currency member states will change to the union in three stages as follows:

Stage 1:
started before the Maastricht Treaty in July 1990. Its main objective was to remove limitations of capital, merchandise, labor, and service flows between member countries.

Stage 2:
effective since January 1994. It intends to deepen the economic and monetary cooperation between member states.

Stage 3:
will begin in January 1999. Countries judged as meeting the requirements provided for in the Maastricht Treaty will enter Stage 3. The main requirements formulated in the treaty are the following:

CHAPTER 11

1. Gross public debt should not exceed 60% of gross domestic product (GDP).
2. Budget sector deficit should not exceed 3% of GDP.
3. Inflation rate during preceeding 12 months should not exceed the average of the three lowest member country inflation rates by more than 1.5 percentage points.
4. Long-term interest rates cannot exceed those of the three countries with the lowest inflation rates by more than 2 percentage points.
5. Exchange rates must be maintained within normal ERM limits for the preceding two years.

Stage 3 means that all participating countries will follow the same monetary and economic policy and that the changeover to a common currency, the euro, will be completed as soon as possible. If this measure proves successful, currency fluctuations and therefore exchange rate rides between member countries will disappear.

It is obvious from the above that currency fluctuations between major countries during the 1950s and 1960s were small. They were therefore a relatively small risk factor in international trade. However, the situation changed dramatically during the 1970s and 1980s when large currency fluctuations became common. The efforts of major central banks to influence exchange rates had only limited effect compared with market forces of supply and demand. The explanation for this fact is that more than one trillion dollars change hands daily, which figure far exceeds the currency reserves of any central bank.

In Finland, the daily currency exchange was approximately 4 billion USD/day in 1995. This equals only three days of total average currency reserve of the Central Bank and is approximately 40 times the daily export value. This proves the dominion of market forces of supply and demand over attempts to control currency fluctuations by the Central Bank.

4 Factors affecting exchange rates

According to the law of one price (see Chapter 11, section 2.3), exchange adjusted prices of identical tradable goods should be equal globally. Exchange rates and purchasing power parity should therefore be based on the trade of manufactured goods. However, only a very small part of the flow of currencies is connected to the trade of goods. In Finland, for example, the daily currency exchange in 1995 of USD 4 billion/day is approximately 40 times the value of daily national exports. This fact demonstrates the lack of connection between flow of goods and flow of currencies. Accordingly, other factors are decisive in forming exchange rates.

The most important factors are the following:
- inflation rates and expectations
- interest rates and expectations
- growth expectations
- political stability.

The impact of currency exchange rates on competitiveness

The following example illustrates two of the factors.
   If the inflation rates in country A and B are 4% and 7%, respectively, the nominal interest rate should then be 3% higher in country B than in country A. If this were not the case, then funds would flow from country B to country A to take advantage of the difference until such time as equilibrium in interest rates would be restored.
   Another way to compensate for the difference in inflation between the two countries would be the devaluation by 3% of country B's currency in relation to that of country A.

In principle, a country with a high inflation rate must have a high interest rate, in order to avoid the flow of funds from the country that would lower its currency reserve. This means lower economic growth and an eventual, theoretical lowering of the value of the currency.

5 Purchasing power parity

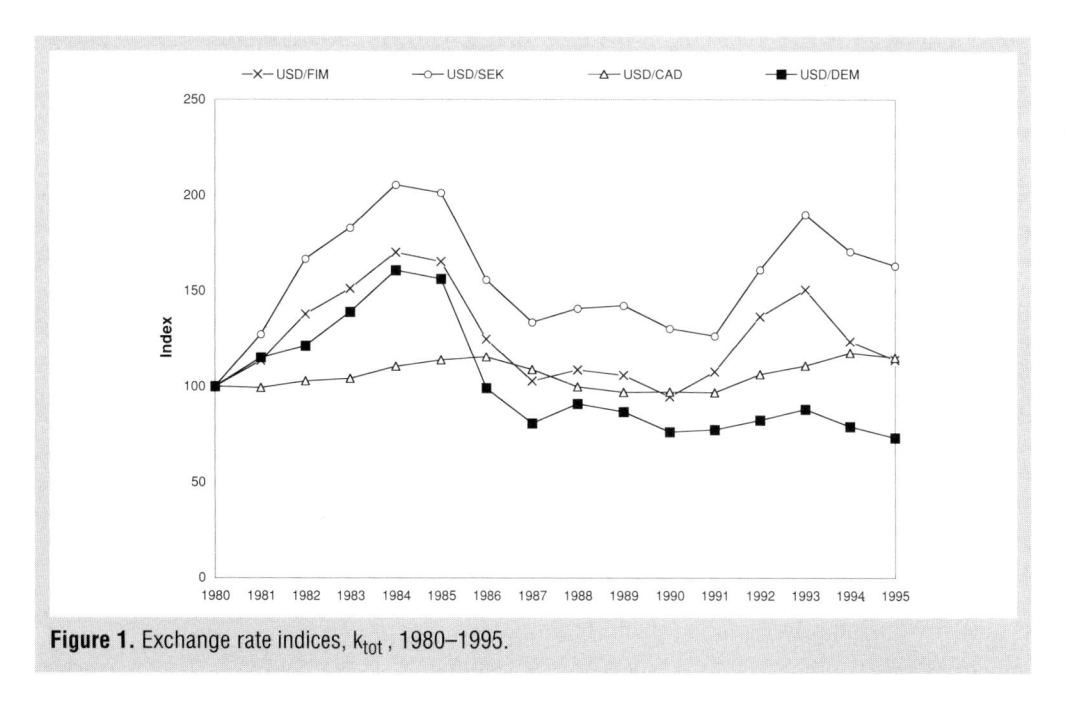

Figure 1. Exchange rate indices, k_{tot}, 1980–1995.

Figure 1 shows the total relative exchange rate fluctuation, k_{tot}, between some countries 1980–1995 in relation to USD. The fluctuations of SEK and FIM have been particularly large. As the base prices of many forest industry products such as long fiber chemical pulp and kraftliner sold in Europe are USD, the fluctuations in this period have greatly influenced the competitiveness of Scandinavian vs. North American producers.
   If the exchange rate variations in Figure 1 had followed purchasing power parity (PPP) accurately as Figure 3 shows, the cost competitiveness of these countries would

CHAPTER 11

have remained stable at exactly the 1980 level. Due to large deviations from PPP in 1980–1995, the cost competitiveness of the entire forest industry and of individual companies varied significantly. Such deviations form a risk factor as analyzed below:

If
i_h is inflation in home country
i_f inflation of foreign country
e_o value of foreign currency in home currency at beginning of period
e_t value of foreign currency in home currency in period t based on PPP
e_r realised value of foreign currency in home currency in period t

$k_{tot} = e_r/e_o$ = total relative currency change during period t

$k_1 = e_t/e_o$ = relative theoretical currency change based on PPP during period t

$k_2 = e_r/e_t$ = relative deviation factor from PPP during period t

$k_{tot} = k_1 \times k_2$ (1)

then
$e_t/e_o = (1 + i_h)^t/(1 + i_f)^t$ or $e_t = e_o ((1 + i_h)^t/(1 + i_f)^t)$ (2)

$e_r = k_2 \times e_t$ (3)

If one uses price indexes such as wholesale price or consumer price indexes, the above equation becomes:

i_f is relative change of price index of foreign country during period t
i_h relative change of price index of home country during period t
$k_1 = i_f/i_h$

$k_2 = k_{tot} (1/k_1) = k_{tot} (i_h/i_f)$ (4)

Table 1 shows the consumer price change in certain countries during 1985–1995. These figures indicate that the inflation rates of the countries have differed radically.

Table 1. Consumer price changes in certain countries during 1985–1995.

Country	Consumer price index 1980	Consumer price index 1995	Annual increase 1980-1995 % per year
Germany	100	154	2.9
USA	100	179	4.0
Canada	100	197	4.6
Finland	100	215	5.2
Sweden	100	255	6.4

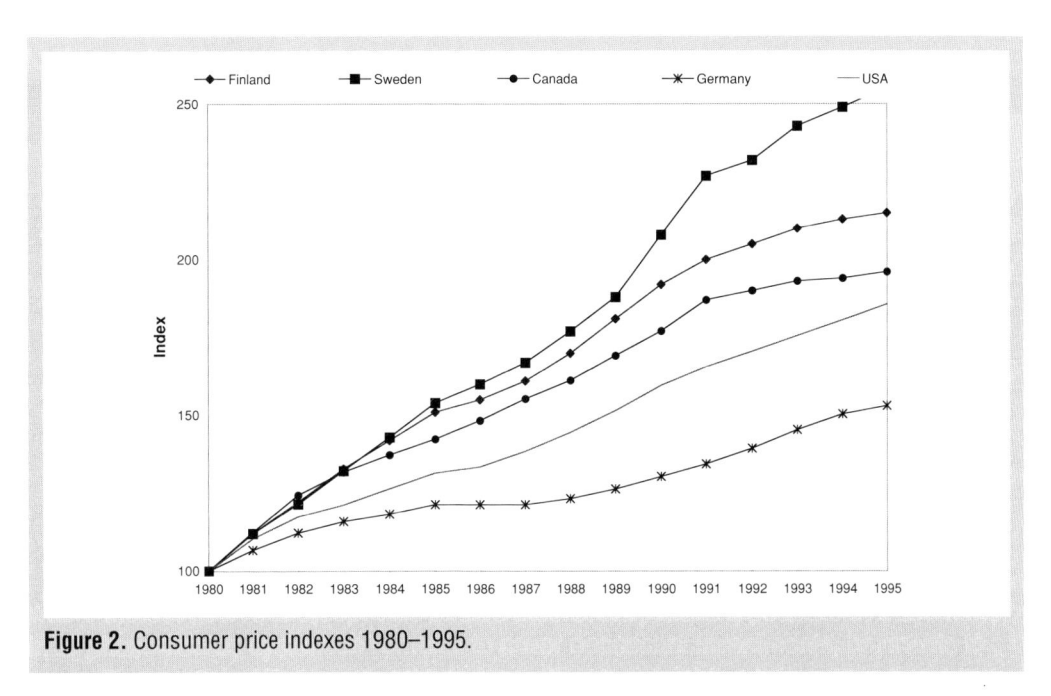

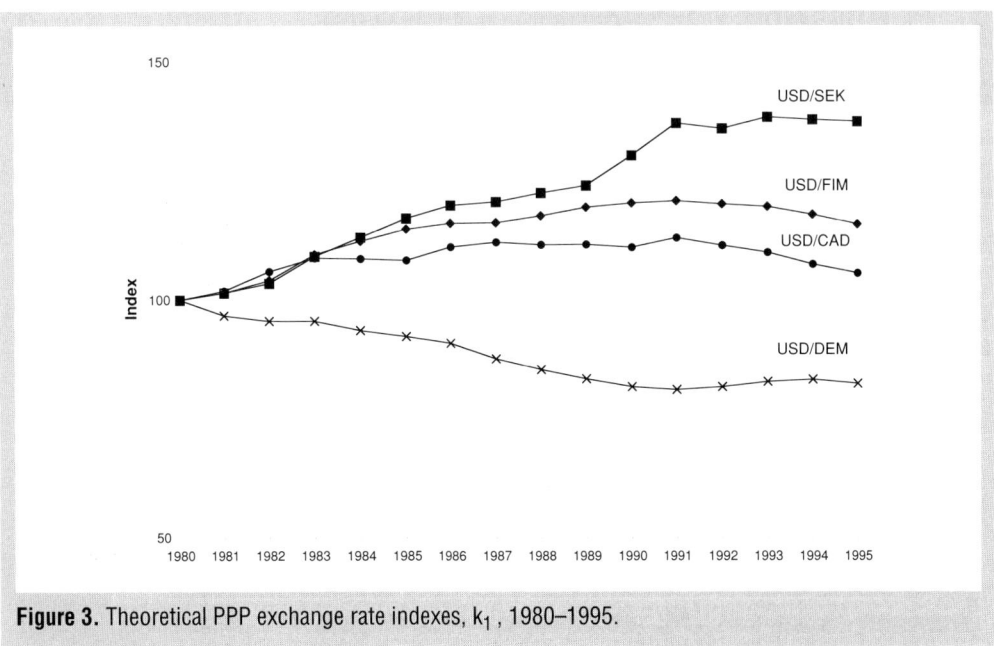

The impact of currency exchange rates on competitiveness

Figure 2. Consumer price indexes 1980–1995.

Figure 3. Theoretical PPP exchange rate indexes, k_1, 1980–1995.

CHAPTER 11

Figure 4. Relative deviation factor from PPP, k_2, 1980–1995.

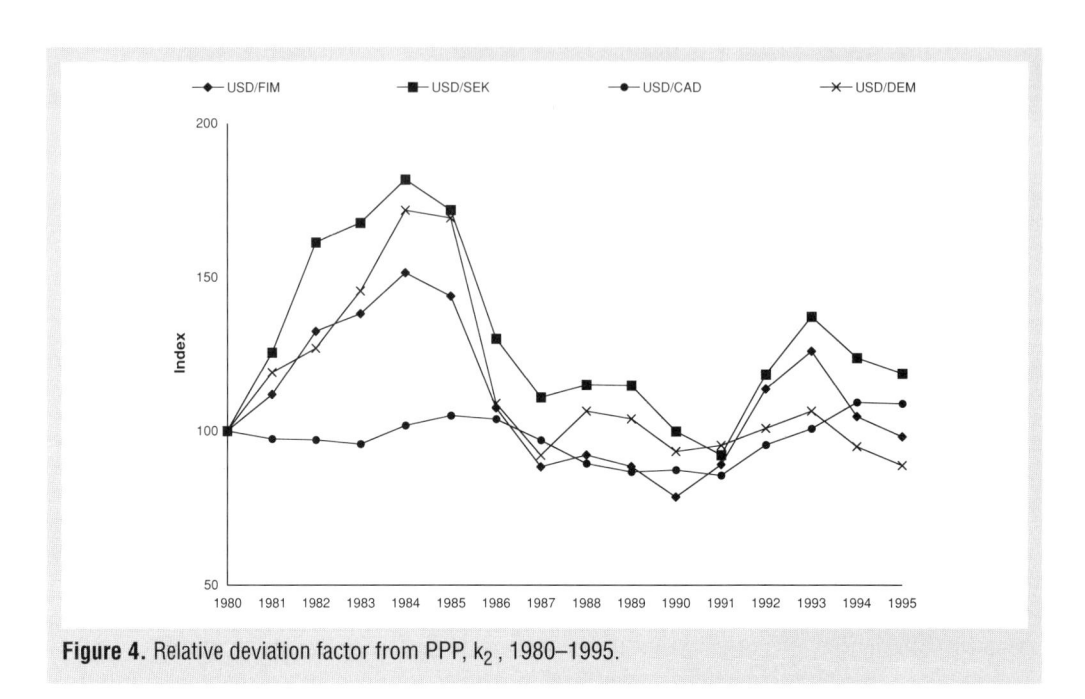

Figure 4 shows the historical k_2 in the above equation and the theoretical currency deviation from PPP (Figure 3). Factor k_1 alone would have required a gradual increase or revaluation of USD in relation to FIM, SEK, and CAD and an equally gradual devaluation in relation to DEM. In reality, the fluctuations have been much stronger particularly in relation to FIM and SEK. One can therefore draw the following conclusions:

1. During 1980–1985, the USD strengthened dramatically against the DEM, SEK, and FIM. This tendency resulted mostly from the deviation from PPP. The strengthening of the USD was due to the economic policy of President Reagan. It consisted of a high interest rate in the United States that caused a high demand for USD with strengthening of the currency as a consequence. The CAD followed the USD closely, which is why there was no major deviation from PPP in this case.

   As a result of the currency developments during 1980–1985, the competitive position of the European forest industry improved dramatically in relation to the North American industry. Sweden with a devaluation of the SEK in the early 1980s particularly gained a more competitive position especially compared with Finland.

2. In 1985, the USD declined in value some 30–40% to restore the PPP close to its 1980 level. During one single year, the competitive position of the North American industry therefore improved radically compared with its European competitors.

3. During 1986–1991, exchange rate movements were fairly moderate. Due to the high inflation rate in Finland compared with the United States and Canada,

the Finnish forest industry had a competitive disadvantage due to negative deviation from 1980 PPP, which in 1990 had reached approximately 20%. During 1986–1990, the Swedish industry also enjoyed a 20–25% advantage over Finland based on the positive PPP deviation from 1980.
4. In 1991 and 1992, the FIM was devalued and allowed to float. This improved the competitive position of the Finnish forest industry. It further strengthened in 1993 when the positive deviation from 1980 PPP level was approximately 25%. In 1994 and 1995, the FIM strengthened to such an extent that the deviation from the 1980 PPP level relative to the United States was practically zero. In 1995, the Swedish industry still enjoyed a 20% positive deviation from PPP relative to the United States and Finland.

6 Conclusions

The following general conclusions result from the above statistics:
- Demand and supply of currencies can cause exchange rate variations and deviations from PPP. The reserves of central banks are too small to have a major impact on exchange rates making market forces the dominant factors.
- Deviations from PPP cause competitive advantages or disadvantages that can be 50% from normal equilibrium, and such situations may last for several years.
- Analysis of cost competitiveness of a given product can give different results due to the above departures from PPP that are dependant on the time of the analysis.
- One cannot predict either changes in exchange rates or deviations from PPP. Later calculation of both can estimate how close to normal a present situation is.
- The reference point for the above statistics is 1980 – a normal year. One could argue that in 1980 the USD and CAD were weak in historical perspective. If this assumption proves correct on the basis of analysis of later years, then the reference point of 1980 as equilibrium is somewhat questionable. All figures for 1980–1995 give an advantage to USD and CAD and a disadvantage to other currencies. The careful selection of the reference point is therefore of major importance.

CHAPTER 11

7 Protective measures against exchange rate variations

7.1 General

It is evident that currency changes can be both very quick and very large. The measures taken to protect a company from the negative consequences of currency variations are called currency hedging.

In most companies the prime rule in currency hedging is to minimize the risk exposure that exchange rate variations cause.

Currency hedging in today's financial markets requires specialized professionals with specialized skills. This chapter therefore only considers the basic principles that apply to the operations of pulp and paper mills.

7.2 Structure of currency position

Forest industry companies that normally export the major part of their production receive their payments in various currencies. This applies especially to Scandinavian companies. Companies in the United States sell much of their produce on the domestic market in local currency. This gives them much less exposure to exchange rate variations.

Receivables in foreign currencies form a receivables or flow position whose volume and internal composition change constantly.

The balance sheet position consists of long-term loans taken in foreign currencies. These are generally more stable.

The following summary shows the impact of currency weakening on the positions indicated above:

1. Receivables position at period t_0:

   A weakening of the domestic currency causes sales to increase when converting receivables to domestic currency. When all the position is in domestic currency usually within 90–120 days, an unexpected extraordinary profit occurs.

   For sales made after the weakening has occurred, the new exchange rates apply. No extra profit will then result.

2. Balance sheet position at period t_0:

   Weakening of the domestic currency causes the value of long-term loans to increase at day one. This means that the increase in value must be entered in the profit and loss account as exchange rate loss to balance the debit and credit in the balance sheet. During the coming months, increased sales and increased profits will compensate the increase in value of long term loans. This usually takes a considerable time.

7.3 Forward selling and buying

The above two methods are probably the most common methods of currency hedging. Forward selling is more common in forest industry companies exporting the majority of their products. Operating mill managers should therefore understand it.

If a forest company sells regularly to Germany at DEM 10 million/month, it needs to secure its future receivables for 6 months ahead against the risk of exchange rate variations. The following measures are necessary as a conceptual example:
1. The company agrees with a bank that today's exchange rate is DEM 1 for FIM 3.0320.
2. The bank borrows 10 million DEM at the prevailing interest rate in Germany of 4.0% at day one.
3. The bank changes 10 million DEM at day one to FIM and receives the prevailing interest rate in Finland of 6.0% for this deposit.
4. The above interest rate differences cause the following exchange rate impact at day 180:
   $((6.0-4.0)\% \times 180 \times 3.0320)/(360 \times 100) = 0.03032$
5. On day 180, the company delivers 10 million DEM to the bank at
   $1 \text{ DEM} = (3.0320 + 0.03032) = 3.06232 \text{ FIM}$.

The bank pays off its debt of 10 million DEM opened at day one. The company receives an extraordinary profit of 303 200 FIM caused by the currency interest rate difference in Germany and Finland.

Forward buying and selling is explained in more detail in Appendix 1.

CHAPTER 11

Appendix 1

The use of forwards and options as a hedging tool

If a forest company sells regularly to a foreign country such as Germany, it can secure the value of its future DEM receivables in FIM against the risk of exchange rate variations by selling the currency to a bank with a forward or buying an option from a bank to sell currency (put option). These two alternatives are described below.

1. Forward selling.

By making a forward contract, the company and the bank agree on an exchange rate for a value date in the future. The forward price is based on the current exchange rate (spot rate) and the interest rate difference of the two currencies.

The forward price is calculated as follows:

$$\text{spot rate} + \frac{\text{spot rate} \times (\text{price currency interest rate} - \text{base currency interest rate}) \times \text{days to maturity}}{100 \times 365}$$

We assume that the company knows that its German sales next month will be DEM 10 million. The company wants to secure the value of its foreign sales for 1 month. If the company sells DEM 10 million to the bank against FIM with the value date being one month (30 days) from the spot date, the forward price is calculated as follows:

We assume that the DEM/FIM spot rate is 3.0000, DEM 1 month interest rate is 3.0% per year and FIM 1 month interest rate is 3.5% per year.

In this example the forward price is

$$\frac{3.0000 \times (3.5 - 3.0) \times 30}{100 \times 365} + \text{spot rate} = 0.001233 + 3.0000 = 3.001233$$

On day 30 the company delivers DEM 10 million to the bank and receives FIM 30 012 330. Thus, it fixed the value of its receivables on a certain level on day one, so it will not gain even if the exchange rate moved in its favor.

2. Buying an option

If the company wants to secure a certain exchange rate for its receivables, but not limit the potential gain if the exchange rates move in its favor, it can buy a put option (option to sell) for a certain premium (price). The option prices are affected by the exchange rate, strike price of the option, the interest rates and the volatility of the currencies.

If we assume the previous exchange and interest rates, and that the one month DEM/FIM volatility is 3.3%, the company could buy a one month DEM 10 million put option with a strike price of 3. 0000 FIM. In fact the company buys a right, but not an obligation to sell DEM 10 million against FIM 30 million, by paying the bank a premium of 0.37% of the amount of the option.

Thus the company has secured, that regardless of the exchange rate on day 30, that it can exercise the option, to sell DEM 10 000 000 and receive FIM 30 000 000. The option premium DEM 37 000 (FIM 111 000) has to be deducted to get the net value of FIM 29 889 000.

If, however the exchange rate has moved in the company's favor, for example to DEM/FIM 3.15, the company gains from the movement, since it can sell the DEM at the prevailing rate, because a put option is only an option, not an obligation, to sell. Thus the net value would be FIM 31 500 00 less FIM 111 000 equalling FIM 31 389 000.

CHAPTER 12

Future strategies for the Scandinavian forest industry

1	**Global trends 1975–1995**	**175**
2	**Western Europe in the mid 1990s**	**176**
2.1	General	176
2.2	Selection of production grades	176
3	**Future trends and outlook for the next century**	**178**
4	**Conclusion**	**179**

Future strategies for the Scandinavian forest industry

1 Global trends 1975–1995

The following factors and trends have had a decisive influence on the development of the forest industry globally during 1975–1995:

1. Paper and board demand has grown by 3% per year. This has been a cornerstone for positive development in the forest industry.
2. Economy of scale has increased the optimum pulp mill and paper machine size in bulk grades by a factor of approximately 2. As a result, the need for financial strength in the investing company, availability of raw materials in terms of both volume and price, and lack of suitable locations have all become more critical and important. These demands have influenced and changed the structure of the forest industry.
3. Recycled fiber has become a widely accepted raw material. Its share of total fiber consumption has increased from 20% to 35%.
4. Latin America has enormous potential to increase its pulp and paper production. It has not conquered the global market in pulp or fine papers. The Latin American share of world paper and board production has increased from 3 to 4% during 1975–1995.
5. The forest industry structure started to become more concentrated in the second half of the 1980s particularly in Europe and Scandinavia. By early 1997, all large Scandinavian companies had acquired or built major facilities in central Europe as part of their international strategy.
   Despite this concentration trend, the forest industry still remains fragmented compared with most other industrial sectors. This factor is likely to have a major impact on the future development of the forest industry.
6. Cyclical patterns have plagued the industry in most grades as a direct result of fragmentation.
7. Asia and the Pacific Rim countries have emerged as large and growing markets. The main local producers have increased their capacity at an astounding rate especially in pulp and woodfree papers. By the mid 1990s the impact of the local Asia and Pacific Rim country producers on a global scale has been small to moderate. This situation is likely to change rapidly.

CHAPTER 12

8. The concept of shareholder value has gained ground significantly in the management of forest industry companies in North America during the 1990s. This trend is expanding to Western Europe.

2 Western Europe in the mid 1990s

2.1 General

Western Europe is the key market area for the Scandinavian forest industry. Approximately 75% of the sales of the Scandinavian forest companies' production is in this region. Continental Europe (Western Europe excluding Scandinavia) is the second largest market area in the world after North America. It is of particular importance to the Scandinavian forest industry.

The following groups compete for market shares in Continental Europe:
1. Domestic, Continental European producers
2. Scandinavian producers
3. Overseas producers
    3.1. North American producers
    3.2. Latin American producers
    3.3. Asia Pacific producers

2.2 Selection of production grades

Continental European producers

The following factors concerning Continental European producers require consideration:
+ low transport costs
+ availability and control of waste paper supplies
+ proximity to customers (short delivery times, easy, close customer contacts, personal relations)

- lack of wood and/or high cost of wood
- tight environmental legislation and control
- structure of the industry fragmented and partly technically outdated

As a result of the above factors, chosen production grades should have a low share of wood costs compared with total manufacturing costs. They should also use recycled fibers, have poor transportability, and a high transport cost share of total costs. Easy access to markets and customers is an additional positive factor.

Using the above analysis, the following grades are highly suitable for production in Continental Europe:
1. Tissue paper and converted tissue products
    - high transport costs
    - suitability of recycled fiber as a raw material
    - easy integration to converting
2. Recovered paper based corrugated raw materials (testliner and wellenstoff) and cartonboards (white-lined chipboard)
    - suitability of recovered paper as a raw material
    - easy integration to converting
3. Recycled newsprint
    - suitability of recovered paper as a raw material
4. Mechanical printing paper (SC and LWC papers)
    - low share of wood costs in total manufacturing costs
    - technically demanding
    - quality advantage of high quality spruce
5. Woodfree papers
    - demanding grade especially in coated papers
    - small end users requiring short delivery times and good customer service
    - possibility to find niche grades where competition from large bulk producers can be avoided.

Overseas producers
    + cheap and abundant raw material supply especially short fiber wood
    + efficient structure of the forest industry

    - exchange rate risks
    - transport and transport costs
    - domestic orientation
    - occasional low quality level
    - no direct relations with end users owing to middlemen and long distance between supplier and customer

The effect of the above factors leads to the choice of grades where the share of wood costs in total manufacturing costs is high, transportability is good, and transport costs low. Market pulp and kraftliner are particularly good, and newsprint also fulfils many criteria.

Scandinavian producers
    + efficient structure of the industry and large company size
    + high level of technical know-how
    + high standard of forest management
    + transportation cost advantage compared with overseas suppliers

- lack of wood and high cost of wood
- lack of industrially-owned forest in Finland
- lack of domestic recovered paper
- high transport costs in comparison to Continental European industry

Due to the above factors, grades that have high wood paying capacity, low wood consumption and high additional value are appropriate. Competitive grades are the same as in Continental Europe with the exception of those whose transportability is critical such as tissue or corrugated board or those using recycled fiber such as tissue, recovered paper based corrugated raw materials and cartonboards, and newsprint.

It is therefore apparent that Scandinavian and Continental European producers compete with each other in many grades such as newsprint, mechanical printing papers, and woodfree papers. To some extent, this confrontation decreased when the Scandinavian producers acquired Continental European capacity in the middle 1990s.

A good strategic approach for the Scandinavian producers would be to retreat gradually from the grades where competition from overseas producers has grown such as market pulp and kraftliner. Overseas producers have a strong competitive position in Continental Europe in these grades. In addition, overseas suppliers can use marginal pricing when exporting to Europe, since Europe is far from their core markets. This further aggravates the competitive situation and strengthens the cyclical nature for Continental European and Scandinavian markets.

Scandinavian companies have considered the consequences of the above scenario. The relative share of kraftliner vs. total paper and board production and that of market pulp vs. total pulp production has declined in Scandinavia during the last few decades.

3 Future trends and outlook for the next century

Global population growth during the twenty-first century should continue. With a low paper and board consumption per capita in many regions of the world, this creates a large global demand potential. Simultaneously, these trends create new pressure on the world's resource base for the pulp and paper industry using fiber base, especially its forest resources. Intelligent management of the resource base is becoming especially critical for global survival.

The growth of the demand for paper and board products should be particularly strong in Asia and considerably slower in Europe and North America. With very rapid increase in production in Asia, this appears to be the megatrend at the turn of the millenium.

Since Asia has a deficit of recycled and softwood fiber resources, it is unlikely that the area will become a major global player in newsprint, mechanical printing and writing papers, kraftpaper, and containerboard. This is a key factor when considering future strategic alternatives in Europe and North America.

The cost of labor in Europe will continue to be high, and the scarcity of wood and high wood costs will naturally lead strategic trends toward using the potentials of coating and chemistry. Assuming that a rapid production growth in Asia materializes, the European pulp and paper industry must have the defense of its core market in Europe as its primary goal. For a European company, becoming a truly global player would also strengthen its competitive position in Europe.

In Scandinavia, the forest industry forms an essential part of the national economies in the region. This is particularly true for Finland where the forest industry is a cornerstone of the country's standard of living. In many other parts of the world, the forest industry is only a small factor in the national economy. Scandinavian forest companies therefore have an additional incentive to grow and develop. The wood resources in Sweden and especially in Finland do not allow further expansion. Scandinavian forest groups will therefore probably continue to expand through internationalization using their high level of technical know-how. The implementation of this strategy will be crucial for their long-term success and future growth. It will result in large investments abroad and smaller domestic investments in the next decade.

Scandinavian companies will still have to maintain the competitiveness of their domestic production facilities in addition to the above internationalization trend. Since a lack of wood raw material will limit capacity expansion, modernization of existing capacity or building new, competitive facilities will require closing down old and obsolete machines and mills. Such measures will in many cases be difficult to implement and will require new skills and entail decisions not necessary earlier.

4 Conclusion

As the year 2000 approaches, the outlook for the pulp and paper industry globally is both interesting and highly challenging. The expected growth in demand during the next decades will mean a dynamic industrial environment. The risks include a few small negative changes influencing development in the direction of stagnation. Such factors might be electronic media cutting some demand for growth in newspapers and magazines, hostility to excessive packaging reducing growth, excessive investments in Asia combined with a smaller regional growth in demand particularly in China, small changes in consumer attitudes, etc.

Successful pulp and paper companies must naturally follow the above positive and negative trends closely and select their strategy so as to benefit from the opportunities and avoid the threats resulting from these trends.

Glossary

The economic terms are explained very briefly in the glossary. They are explained more properly in Table 2, Chapter 7.

BHKP	Bleached Hardwood Kraft Pulp
Boxboard	Paperboard used to fabricate boxes, see also Folding boxboard.
BSKP	Bleached Softwood Kraft Pulp
Capital employed	Total assets - interest free liabilities
Capital turnover	Sales divided by total assets
Cartonboards	Cartonboards are used for packaging boxes and consist of two or more layers. The outer layer is usually from chemical pulp, and the middle layers either from mechanical pulp (FBB) or recycled fiber (WLC). Both coated and uncoated cartonboards are produced.
Cash flow	EBIT + depreciation - financial expenses, taxes and change in working capital
CEPAC	European Confederation of Pulp, Paper and Board Industries (see CEPI)
CEPI	Confederation of European Paper Industries
Chemical pulp	Pulp obtained by digestion of wood with various chemicals. The separation of fibers is accomplished by dissolving away the lignin to release the intact fibers. The two major types of chemical pulp are sulphate (Kraft) pulp and sulphite pulp.
Coated woodfree paper (CWF)	Coated fine paper
Containerboard	Same as Corrugated raw/case materials
Corrugated board	Consists of one or more layers of rippled paper (fluting) glued to one layer or between several layers of flat paper (liner).
Corrugated raw/case materials	A collective term for different paper grades (kraftliner, testliner and fluting) used in the production of corrugated board. Same as containerboard.
Deflated sales	Real value of sales, e.g. value of 1985 sales in 1995 money.
Deinking	Removal of ink and other extraneous material from waste paper.
Depreciation	A bookkeeping transaction which should cover the wear and tear of an investment made earlier.
Digester	A vessel used to treat cellulosic raw material with chemicals under pressure and temperature to produce pulp. It may be designed for either batch or continuous operation.
DIP	(Deinked Pulp) The pulp resulting from the deinking of waste paper.

Glossary

Dry-end	That part of the paper machine where the paper is dried, calendered and reeled.
EBIT	Earnings Before Interest and Taxes, same as operating profit.
EBITD	Earnings Before Interest, Taxes and Depreciation, same as gross profit.
EPS	Earnings Per Share - See also formula 7.6.
FAO	Food and Agriculture Organization of the United Nations.
Felt	Continuous belt made of wool, cotton or synthetic fibers. It is used to mechanically convey the wet sheet, provide a cushion for the sheet between press rolls and serve as a medium through which water is removed. In addition, it provides power transmission to various rolls in the press section.
Fiber wood	Wood which is usually too small, of inferior quality or the wrong species to be used in the manufacture of lumber or plywood.
Fine paper	High quality printing and writing paper produced from bleached chemical pulp, either coated or uncoated. Same as woodfree paper.
Fluting	Rippled middle layer of corrugated board produced from semi-chemical pulp (SC fluting) or recycled fiber (Wellenstoff).
Folding boxboard (FBB)	Paperboard produced from mechanical pulp, with one surface made from chemical pulp. Packaging uses include food, cigarettes and cosmetics.
GDP	Gross Domestic Product.
Gravure printing	A method of printing utilizing a plate or cylinder with minute engraved or etched depressions on the surface to hold ink and then transfer the ink to a paper surface.
Groundwood	(or Stone Groundwood) Mechanical pulp produced in a process in which pulpwood blocks are ground into pulp at atmospheric pressure.
Hardwood (HW)	Wood from broad-leaved trees such as birch and eucalyptus (short fibers).
Headbox	That part of the paper machine which receives the stock and transforms the pipeline flow into a uniform rectangular flow equal in width to the paper machine and at uniform velocity in the machine direction.
Investment rate / level	Total investments divided by sales
Kraftliner	Kraft linerboard, outer layer of corrugated board produced from virgin fiber.
Liner	Outer and inner layers of corrugated board. See also kraftliner and testliner.
Liquid packaging board (LPB)	Paperboard used in the packaging of milk and fruit juices. LPB consists of several layers of paper pressed together and treated to make it impermeable.
Log / Sawlog	Wood which is used in the manufacture of lumber.
Long fiber	See softwood.
Lumber	(Same as Timber) Product of a sawmilling operation.

LWC paper	(Light Weight Coated) Coated super-calandered paper used mainly in consumer magazines, catalogues and advertising material. LWC paper is made from a blend of mechanical and bleached chemical pulp.
M & A's	Mergers and Acquisitions.
Market pulp	Non-integrated pulp sold on the world market. It is mostly bleached sulphate pulp (chemical pulp). It can be divided into softwood and hardwood pulp.
Mechanical papers	Paper grades made of mechanical pulp, e.g. SC, LWC and Newsprint.
Mechanical pulp	Any pulp produced by mechanical methods (using mechanical energy and/or methods to separate the fibers).
NBSKP	Northern Bleached Softwood Kraft Pulp.
Newsprint	Paper used in newspaper publishing, traditionally it has been made largely from mechanical pulp but nowadays increasingly from waste paper.
NSSC fluting	Neutral sulphite semi-chemical fluting.
OECD	Organization for Economic Cooperation and Development.
Offset printing	Any printing method in which the image is transferred to a rubber-covered blanket which, in turn, transfers the image to the paper.
Operating margin	EBIT divided by Sales.
Operating profit	EBIT.
OTC paper	One-time carbonized paper.
PE-ratio	Price per Earnings ratio, share price divided by earnings per share. See also formula 7.7.
R & D	Research and Development.
Recovery boiler	Water tube boiler which utilizes concentrated black liquor or other chemical pulping waste liquor as the principal fuel.
Recovery rate	Recycled fiber collection divided by paper and board consumption.
ROCE	Return On Capital Employed.
ROE	Return On Equity.
ROI	Return On Investment.
Sackpaper	Paper manufactured from sulphate pulp. It has high strength and is used for production of paper sacks.
SC paper	(Super Calandered paper) A high-glaze uncoated printing paper made largely from mechanical pulp. SC is usually used in consumer magazines and advertising material.
Short fiber	See hardwood.
Softwood (SW)	Wood from trees characterised by having needles such as spruce or pine (long fibers).
Solid bleached board (SBB)	High quality paperboard produced from chemical pulp. It is characterized by its purity and good printability. Packaging uses include perfume, chocolates, pharmaceuticals and cigarettes.

Glossary

Testliner	Recycled linerboard, outer layer of corrugated board produced from recycled fiber.
Tissue	A paper used for hygienic purposes like toilet paper, napkins and kitchen towels. The proportion of recycled fiber in the furnish of tissue is high and increasing.
TMP	(Thermomechanical Pulp) A pulp produced by a thermomechanical process in which the chips are softened by steaming under pressure prior to a pressurized refining stage.
Trim	Width of finished paper produced on a paper machine.
Utilization rate	Recycled fiber consumption divided by paper and board production.
Wellenstoff	Rippled middle layer of corrugated board produced from recycled fiber.
Wet-end	That portion of the paper machine which includes the headbox, wire part and press section.
White lined chipboard (WLC)	Paperboard produced from recycled fiber. WLC is used in the packaging of washing powders, dry food and toys.
Wire	Endless belt of woven wire cloth for the drainage of stock and forming of a fiber web. Usually made of metal and/or plastic.
Woodfree paper (WF)	Same as fine paper.
Working capital	Accounts receivable + inventories - accounts payable.

Sources

Gary A. Smook Handbook of Pulp & Paper Terminology - A Guide To Industrial and Technological Usage

American Paper Institute The Dictionary of Paper - 4th edition

Salomon Brothers Product Glossary

Conversion factors

To convert numerical values found in this book in the RECOMMENDED FORM, divide by the indicated number to obtain the values in CUSTOMARY UNITS. This table is an excerpt from TIS 0800-01 "Units of measurement and conversion factors." The complete document containing additional conversion factors and references to appropriate TAPPI Test Methods is available at no charge from TAPPI, Technology Park/Atlanta, P. O. Box 105113, Atlanta GA 30348-5113 (Telephone: +1 770 209-7303, 1-800-332-8686 in the United States, or 1-800-446-9431 in Canada).

Property	To convert values expressed in RECOMMENDED FORM	Divide by	To obtain values expressed In CUSTOMARY UNITS
Area	square centimeters [cm^2]	6.4516	square inches [in^2]
	square meters [m^2]	0.0929030	square feet [ft^2]
	square meters [m^2]	0.8361274	square yards [yd^2]
	square meters [m^2]	4046.86	acres
	square kilometers [km^2]	0.01	hectares [ha]
	square kilometers [km^2]	2.58999	square miles [mi^2]
Length	nanometers [nm]	0.1	angstroms [D]
	micrometers [Fm]	1	microns
	millimeters [mm]	0.0254	mils [mil or 0.001 in]
	millimeters [mm]	25.4	inches [in]
	meters [m]	0.3048	feet [ft]
	kilometers [km]	1.609	miles [mi]
Mass	grams [g]	28.3495	ounces [oz]
	kilograms [kg]	0.453592	pounds [lb]
	metric tons (tonne) [t] (= 1000 kg)	0.907185	tons (= 2000 lb)
Mass per unit area	grams per square meter [g/m^2]	3.7597	pounds per ream, 17 x 22 - 500
	grams per square meter [g/m^2]	1.4801	pounds per ream, 25 x 38 - 500
	grams per square meter [g/m^2]	1.4061	pounds per ream, 25 x 40 - 500
	grams per square meter [g/m^2]	4.8824	pounds per 1000 square feet [$lb/1000\ ft^2$]
	grams per square meter [g/m^2]	1.6275	pounds per 3000 square feet [$lb/3000\ ft^2$]
	grams per square meter [g/m^2]	1.6275	pounds per ream, 24 x 36 - 500
Speed	meters per second [m/s]	0.30480	feet per second [ft/s]
	millimeters per second [mm/s]	5.080	feet per minute [ft/min or fpm]
Volume, solid	cubic centimeters [cm^3]	16.38706	cubic inches [in^3]
	cubic meters [m^3]	0.0283169	cubic feet [ft^3]
	cubic meters [m^3]	0.764555	cubic yards [yd]

Index

A
acquisitions 91–94, 96, 98

C
competitiveness 128–129, 133–136
concentration.... 13, 77–78, 87, 90–91, 96
cost structure 102, 117, 122
currency fluctuations 162, 164
currency hedging...................... 170–171

D
devaluation................ 162–163, 165, 168
drain 24

E
economy.. 147
economy of scale........ 141–142, 144–149
exchange rate variations 160, 165, 169–170, 172
exports   22, 23–24, 27

F
financial integration........................... 152
financial results 97
Finland 21–27
forest area............. 32, 35, 37, 39, 41–45
forest increment 24
forest industry structure...................... 78

G
growth 10–11, 14–18

H
horizontal integration........................ 152

I
investment decision 127–130, 136
investment level 103, 108, 113
investment rate 14
investments........................... 25, 26

M
main producers 87–90, 94, 96
mergers 91–96, 98
minimills 147

O
opportunities................................... 15

P
paper market................................... 61
price trends 69–71
production volumes...................... 21–23
profitability . 103–104, 106–108, 111, 113, 117, 119, 121–123

R
recovery rate 49, 52–55, 57
revaluation....................... 162–163, 168
risks....................................... 127, 136

S
Scandinavia 30, 41
shareholder value.............. 108–110, 118

T
threats 16

V
value based management............ 110, 118
vertical integration............. 152–154, 157

W
wood costs 31–32, 36–37, 41, 44